GameDay
The Untold Story of America's Game

Tim Cooper

Copyright © 2023 Willard & Arthur Books

All rights reserved.

ISBN: 9798865143451

DEDICATION

To my family- my wife, April, and our incredible kids, Makayla, Trace and Lilly Grace. Thanks for watching hours of college football with me while engaging in the joy, heartbreak, celebration and desperation that is the pageantry of the game we love.

CONTENTS

	Introduction	1
1	A New Ballgame	5
2	The Father of American Football	15
3	Blood, Sweat & Hate	26
4	Leatherheads	34
5	Jim Thorpe	42
6	Something To Play For	49
7	Knute Rockne, All American	56
8	The Game Survives	65
9	A Barrier To Be Broken	79
10	The Bear	90
11	Television & The Worldwide Leader	101
12	Heisman	113
13	September 11	124
14	A New Era	133
	Resources	138
	About The Author	139

INTRODUCTION

"For every winner, there's a loser, and that person didn't really need to lose. They just didn't understand the gameplan."
Buzz Aldrin

When you turn left onto Overlake Avenue the first thing you notice is the street is adorned with massive southern live oak trees. One of those trees engulfed my new backyard as I saw the house for the first time. The legend of the tree was said to be more than 100 years old and took six men to surround and encircle the base.

I was eight years old when we moved to Orlando, Florida, from Bedford, Indiana. I came from the hot bed of High School Basketball, but I was a Kentucky Wildcat fan when it came to college athletics. My father was a High School Basketball star in south central Kentucky and went on to play College Basketball.

It's funny the things you remember as a kid. I can remember boxes. I can remember my new neighbors. I can remember riding my bike for the first time in a suburb (we lived in the country in Indiana and my explorations were limited to our church parking lot).

One of the things I remember vividly is my father constructing a basketball goal for me in the backyard under the shade of that oak tree. I couldn't have been happier. I loved basketball. I had my own kingdom to dribble, shoot and act out my NCAA Final Four dreams while inviting my new friends to come act out their dreams as well.

A funny thing happened.

I fell in love with college football.

Nobody in my neighborhood wanted to play basketball. They all wanted to play football. I soon found myself playing tackle football on our thick St. Augustine grass in our front yard instead of working on my crossover under the shade tree.

Where I came from football was something that happened while you talked about basketball's approach.

When I moved to Florida, I found out that football was something you talked about year-round.

We didn't watch football. We played it. Unless you were a Notre Dame fan it was difficult to follow your team on TV in the 1980s. We played a lot of football in my yard and my friend's yards. We played football at recess at school. Imagine a school today allowing a tackle football game during recess. There were some wonderful things about the 1980s.

I truly fell in love with college football in the most painful way possible 5 years after moving to Florida.

It was Saturday, September 11, 1993.

My Kentucky Wildcats were hosting the Florida Gators and the game was on national television.

Bragging rights with all my friends were on the line.

Kentucky intercepted Florida seven times that day and launched the career of Florida Quarterback Danny Wuerffel all at the same time. After the starter, Terry Dean, threw 4 interceptions, the old ball coach, Steve Spurrier, went with reserve QB Wuerffel. He went on to throw 3 interceptions himself but with 3 seconds on the clock he connected with Chris Doering for a touchdown to lift the Gators to a 24-20 victory as time expired.

I remember falling on the couch. It wasn't the last time I would be heartbroken by University of Kentucky football. I knew that my heart hurt. In fact, I was just as heartbroken as I had been when Kentucky lost a basketball game on a last second shot in the NCAA tournament a year earlier.

That's the point I knew it.

I was in love with college football.

College Football has had a profound impact on the United States. Regional rivalries, legends, folklore, and economic engines all revolve around the game.

In 2019, NCAA Division I athletics programs brought in a combined $15.8 billion of revenue. A quick glimpse at the top ten revenue generating schools will show you how much college football matters to the bottom line of college athletics:

1. Ohio State - $251 Million
2. Texas - $239 Million
3. Alabama - $214 Million
4. Michigan - $210 Million
5. Georgia - $203 Million
6. LSU - $199 Million
7. Texas A&M - $193 Million
8. Florida - $190 Million
9. Penn State - $181 Million
10. Oklahoma - $177 Million

Every team on the list is a NCAA Division I football powerhouse. Television contracts, corporate sponsorships, ticket sales, concessions, marketing contracts and more have created one of the largest industries in the United States.

College Football revenue is second only to that of the National Football League (NFL) in the United States. Football is the king of American sports whether the writers of Cooperstown or the disciples of Springfield, Massachusetts, want to admit it. Where did it come from? How did football grip an entire country and carve out an incredible industry?

In many ways, football is America's game. We didn't borrow it although its roots are found in a familiar global game (but not the one you think). We didn't copy it. There is no British College Football.

No- the pageantry on display for 12 weeks a year in the Fall belongs to us.

The game has a rich history that is woven together with that of the nation which founded it.

From the Civil War to the Steel Towns of the Midwest. From the Dust Bowls of The Great Depression to the battlefields of World War II. From The Civil Rights Movement to Campus Protests. From tragedy to 9/11 and beyond.

Whether you Roll Tide or you OH-IO. Whether you are a Michigan Man or a War Eagle. Whether you do the Gator Chomp or the Seminole Chop. This story is for you because it is our story. The story of College Football is The American Story.

1 A NEW BALLGAME

"The art of war is simple enough. Find out where your enemy is. Get at him as soon as you can. Strike him as hard as you can and keep moving on."
Ulysses S. Grant

They lined country roads as far as the eye could see. No longer marching in rows or columns. The weathered and worn veterans of the Civil War limped their way home across the country. Each fork in the road divided the groups until they found themselves as individuals walking down a familiar home stretch.

The American Civil War raged from 1861 to 1865 and stands as one of the most tumultuous periods in the nation's history. It remains the deadliest war in American history. 360,222 Union soldiers and 258,000 Confederate soldiers were buried or left lying in cornfields, strewn across creek beds, propped against plank fences and lining the roads. Mark Twain captured the enormous stretch of the war when he said:

"The Civil War created an extraordinary situation. It was fought on farms and in towns, and in homes. It was fought by ragged individuals and by neatly uniformed armies. It was fought on horseback and on riverboats. It was a picture gallery of a thousand perspectives."

In the wake of the American Civil War, the nation faced a myriad of challenges, including the reconstruction of the South, the integration of millions of freed slaves to society, and the need for educational reforms. During this critical period, a profound transformation took place in the realm of higher education, particularly with regards to the participation of men. The post-Civil War era witnessed a notable surge in the enrollment of men in colleges across the United States, signifying a pivotal moment in the country's educational history.

Before the Civil War, access to higher education was primarily reserved for the affluent and privileged, limiting opportunities for the majority of the population. However, with the conclusion of the war, there emerged a growing realization of the necessity for a more inclusive and accessible education system. The establishment of the Morrill Land-Grant Acts in 1862 and 1890, which allocated federal lands to states for the purpose of creating institutions that focused on agriculture, mechanics, and military science, played a crucial role in expanding educational opportunities for men from diverse socio-economic backgrounds.

The post-war era also witnessed a shift in societal attitudes towards education, with an increasing recognition of the importance of knowledge and skills in rebuilding the nation. As the country transitioned from an agrarian to an industrial economy, the demand for specialized skills and expertise grew exponentially, prompting more men to seek higher education to secure better employment opportunities. The burgeoning industrial sector required a skilled workforce, and colleges became crucial hubs for fostering the necessary technical and intellectual capabilities.

Moreover, the recognition of education as a means to promote social mobility fueled the aspirations of men from diverse backgrounds, leading to a surge in enrollment in colleges across the country. Men sought to improve their social and economic standing, recognizing that education was a key pathway to achieving these goals.

The post-Civil War era marked a turning point in the history of higher education in the United States, with men increasingly recognizing the importance of pursuing college education for personal and societal advancement. The expansion of educational opportunities, coupled with shifting societal attitudes, laid the foundation for a more inclusive and dynamic educational landscape that would shape the future of the nation.

As the country was torn apart by political, social, and economic divides, young men across the country sought ways to form the bond they felt in uniform, as well as the need to exercise aggression. College campuses across the country soon began to adopt athletic teams as a way for young men to compete for their campus pride in much the same way they identified with their state or town during the war.

The ante-bellum period- referring to the period prior to The Civil War- provided a much more regulated, if not military, campus experience. There was little activity or time devoted to any type of athletic programs on campus. Historian Guy Lewis wrote:

The ante-bellum campus was almost devoid of sport. Students had not learned to play with seriousness of purpose and faculty had not discovered that the collegiate experience should consist of more than intellectual development and moral improvement. Student life was dull, Spartan, well-regulated and academically rigorous. Austere faculty members, usually former clergymen, exercised complete control over every aspect of the lives of their charges. They generally regarded play as a waste of time but permitted it unless the activity became too offensive. But then, students were not very interested in playing games.

It was inevitable following a culture shaping event such as The Civil War that young men would once more seek to participate and compete together. Sports began to emerge in the post-Civil War void. Basketball was invented by Dr. James Naismith in 1891. Baseball, known as "rounders," had been around for decades but now began to grow on campuses. One of the sports to emerge and explode on campuses early during those Reconstruction Years was called football.

159,165 men and boys from Massachusetts served in The Civil War. 133,002 men served in the Army Infantry while 26,163 served in the Navy. 13% of the entire population of the state fought in the war. The state would lose 13,000 of those men in the conflict. Of the young men who returned and were of schooling age, many would enroll in the multiple universities within the state of Massachusetts and neighboring Connecticut. It was on many of these campuses that the game of football would take root and grow.

The game was unique. It had varying rules depending on where you played it. Many schools kicked the ball like soccer. Some teams held the ball and had scrums like rugby. No one dared throw the ball through the air. The rules often were agreed upon prior to a match. The only consistent standard across the board was the desire for young men to carry the ball and hit the opponent.

College football, with its growing popularity and ability to unify people during a time of national crisis, played a significant role in post-Civil War culture. It provided a glimmer of hope, a respite from the chaos, and a symbol of unity in a country torn apart by division. The sport's ability to bring people together across political and geographical lines underscores the power of sports in times of adversity. College football following the Civil War reminds us that even in the darkest moments of history, the human spirit can find solace and connection in the joy of competition and the bonds of shared interests.

The year 1869 marked a pivotal moment in the history of American sports. On a crisp autumn day just 4 years after the end of the Civil War, in New Brunswick, New Jersey, two prestigious colleges, Princeton and Rutgers, gathered for a historic event that would forever alter the course of athletic competition in the United States. This event would serve as both the first college football game and college soccer game in America, a seminal moment that birthed a beloved national pastime.

In the late 19th century, the American sporting landscape was vastly different from what we know today. The game played on that November 6th afternoon was far removed from the highly organized, meticulously regulated sport of modern American football. There were no helmets, no goalposts, and no yard markers. The field was a sprawling 120 yards long, and teams consisted of 25 players each. Rules were rudimentary, closer to a mix of soccer and rugby than contemporary football.

This pioneering contest followed a set of rules known as the "Rutgers Rules." Under these guidelines, the objective was simple: get the ball over the opponent's goal line, whether by running with it or kicking it. Scoring was modest, with each goal worth just one point. In contrast to modern football, where specialized positions and elaborate strategies are common, the players of 1869 were a diverse group, representing various athletic backgrounds.

The game itself was a historic spectacle. Despite the relatively primitive conditions and a meager crowd of spectators, Rutgers and Princeton's clash demonstrated the inherent appeal of football. Rutgers emerged as the victor, winning 6-4. They scored the game's only two goals, while Princeton managed four "rouges.". The outcome was less about winning or losing, but more about the birth of a new sporting tradition.

The 1869 Princeton vs. Rutgers game marked a watershed moment in American sports history. The game ignited a spark of interest in football that rapidly spread to other colleges and universities across the country. Soon, schools like Harvard, Yale, and Columbia began fielding their own football teams and adapting rules to suit their needs. It was the inception of intercollegiate football as we know it today.

The game spread like wildfire as did the number of schools fielding teams. Most would expect to find the origins of football in South Bend, Indiana, or Tuscaloosa, Alabama. Perhaps in Ann Arbor, Michigan, or Columbus, Ohio. In truth- the game found its humble beginnings in places like Medford, Massachusetts, on the campus of Tufts University.

The year 1875 witnessed another significant milestone in the early history of American intercollegiate football. The football game played between Harvard and Tufts Universities on June 4, 1875, was not only a pivotal moment in the development of college football but also an intriguing example of how the sport was evolving in the United States during this era. It is commonly referred to as The Game.

The Harvard-Tufts football game of 1875 took place at Jarvis Field in Cambridge, Massachusetts, and was one of the earliest recorded football contests between two American colleges. The rules for this game were still evolving, and the form of football played then also differed markedly from the contemporary version.

American football had still yet to fully develop its modern rules and structure. The sport was still more akin to a hybrid of rugby and soccer. In the case of the Harvard-Tufts game, the teams followed a variant of rugby football rules, which allowed for a mix of carrying and kicking the ball opposed to only kicking as had occurred in the Princeton vs. Rutgers game of 1869.

The game itself was a spirited and competitive affair, featuring teams from two prominent institutions. While precise details of the match are limited, historical accounts suggest that the game ended in a 1-0 victory for Tufts. The scoring system utilized was one point per goal. Tuft's victory marked one of the early successes in its football history.

The Harvard-Tufts football game of 1875 was yet another early example of intercollegiate athletic competition in the United States. While it may seem primitive by today's standards, this historic encounter played a pivotal role in the evolution of American football. It demonstrated the growing popularity of football as a collegiate sport and contributed to the ongoing refinement of rules and regulations.

This game was a steppingstone in the journey towards the organized and widely celebrated American football we know today. It serves as a reminder of the sport's humble beginnings and its remarkable transformation into a beloved national pastime that continues to captivate fans and athletes alike. If you visit the College Football Hall of Fame in South Bend, Indiana, you will find a team photo of the 1875 Tufts University team that commemorates the victory and the significance of the game.

Tufts would find itself at the center of both college

Yale University Football Team

football and American history once again in 1913. The cold rainy fall day featured a much-anticipated matchup with Army. The Army halfback was creating a stir across the college football world of the northeast and onlookers came to get their glimpse. He played both ways and had even managed to tackle the amazing Jim Thorpe the week prior. The crowd gasped as the Army halfback went down with a knee injury that he would never recover from as he played the last college football game of his career. He would later say that the knee injury altered the course of his life. Little did the amazing crowd that day know that they were watching future World War II hero and President of the United States of America- Dwight D. Eisenhower.

Tufts University did not hold the rights to all early College Football action. Yale University has claim to some of the most significant developments of college football. A storied academic institution, the 1880s marked a pivotal period for Yale's football program, as it secured multiple national championships during this decade.

The 1880s were a transformative time for American football. The sport was still in its infancy, and its rules were in a state of flux. Prior to this decade, football was a rough, violent game more closely resembling rugby than modern American football. However, in 1880, Yale played a crucial role in codifying the rules of the game and shaping the sport into a safer and more organized activity.

During the 1880s, Yale University's football team established itself as a dominant force in the sport. The team won several championships, cementing its reputation as a football powerhouse. Notable national championship victories for Yale in this decade include those in 1888, 1891, and 1892. These championships were achieved through a combination of strong coaching, talented athletes, and the innovative rule changes that Yale helped introduce.

There was also another component to the Yale success- the newly important Coach. The role was filled by a former star player with an innovative mind. His success still reverberates throughout the game today. There is no surprise that Walter Camp became known as The Father of American Football.

2 THE FATHER OF AMERICAN FOOTBALL

"Play fair, but play hard; win if you can, lose if you must- but take your victories modestly and your whippings without a whimper!"
Walter Camp

When Nicholas Camp boarded his transport for the New World from Nazeing, Essex, England, in 1630, he had no idea his decision would impact an annual multibillion-dollar industry for centuries to come. The average trip across the Atlantic Ocean from England to the newly founded colony of Massachusetts took 69 days on average. It was ravaged with danger, illness, mutinies and often starvation for those ships with undisciplined crews in the newly established industry of trans-Atlantic travel. It was not uncommon for less reputable liners and crews to raid the passenger storehouse and consume their rations when hunger first struck. The end-result was a miserable starvation for many who attempted the trip. It was a new journey to a new land that was still developing as an industry.

During the 1600s, various factors propelled individuals to undertake the daunting voyage from England to Massachusetts. Religious persecution, economic hardships, and the pursuit of new opportunities were among the primary drivers. Many settlers sought religious freedom, escaping the religious turmoil and restrictions prevalent in England, and aspired to establish communities where they could practice their faith without fear of persecution. The promise of economic prosperity, coupled with the allure of uncharted territories and the prospect of acquiring land, enticed numerous individuals and families to venture across the Atlantic in pursuit of a better life.

Upon reaching Massachusetts, the settlers faced the formidable task of establishing viable communities in an unfamiliar and often hostile environment. The challenges included building suitable housing, cultivating the land, and forging relationships with the indigenous peoples. The establishment of the Massachusetts Bay Colony and other settlements marked the beginning of a new chapter in the region's history, as the immigrants sought to create societies based on their religious beliefs and cultural values. Despite the difficulties, the perseverance and resilience of the settlers laid the groundwork for the development of a thriving and dynamic colonial society in Massachusetts.

Massachusetts itself was new as well. The King granted a royal charter to the Massachusetts Bay Company establishing the settlement of the territory on March 19, 1628. It was the first charter of the New World. Explorers, Adventurers, Farmers, Businessmen, Religious men and Criminals alike, all sought to make their mark on the New World. Nicholas Camp had no idea of the mark he made.

Walter Chauncey Camp was born on April 7, 1859, in New Britain, Connecticut, nearly 230 years after his ancestor from Nazeing, Essex, England, made the harrowing journey across the Atlantic Ocean. He attended Hopkins Grammar School in New Haven and entered Yale College (now Yale University) in 1875. As a member of Delta Kappa Epsilon and the famed Skull and Bones, he attended Yale Medical School from 1880 to 1883 upon his undergraduate completion. A Typhoid Fever pandemic in the 1880s would alter the course of his life and millions of others.

Camp played football during his undergraduate days and was intrigued by the lack of standards compared to his medical studies. In the early 1870's (the exact date is disputed), he attended a meeting with representatives from the prestigious academic institutions of Columbia, Rutgers, Princeton and Yale Universities. This meeting was the foundation and beginning of the Intercollegiate Football Association (IFA). The IFA was one of the earliest college football rules and scheduling organizations. The goal was to standardize the game and how it was played.

Camp was a versatile athlete during his collegiate career, excelling in track and field, baseball, and rugby football during his college years. However, it was his involvement in rugby football that set the stage for his enduring impact on American football.

Not a particularly large man at only 156 pounds during his playing career he drew attention to himself amongst his much larger teammates. A Harvard College player once famously asked Yale captain Gene Baker, who would go on to become one of the largest land developers in California state history, "You don't mean to let that child play, do you? He will get hurt."

Yet play he did. Camp was known for his athleticism and toughness. As a leader for the program, it was only natural that he would be offered the role of Coach when it became available. It was in that role as Coach that Walter Chauncey Camp would become The Father of American Football some 260 years after his ancestor boarded an unsure charter for the New World.

In the late 19th century, rugby football and association football (soccer) were the dominant forms of football in the United States. Walter Camp played a significant role in promoting rugby football, but he also recognized the need for a standardized set of rules to distinguish American football from its rugby and soccer counterparts.

Camp's influence on the game began to take shape in the 1870s when he proposed several rule changes to make rugby football more suited to American tastes. These changes included introducing the line of scrimmage, the snap from center, and a set of downs. The line of scrimmage was a particularly groundbreaking concept that laid the foundation for the distinctiveness of American football. It created a clear separation between offense and defense, allowing for more strategic plays and a safer game.

In 1880, Walter Camp published his first set of rules for American football, which significantly differed from rugby and soccer. His rules were widely adopted, and they helped transform the game into something uniquely American. Over the next two decades, Camp continued to refine the rules- contributing to the development of the forward pass, the modern scoring system, and other fundamental aspects of American football that still exist today and has helped make the game a multi-billion-dollar industry.

Walter Camp's impact on football extended beyond rulemaking. As the prominent football coach at Yale, he played a key role in developing the concept of football as a team sport. His coaching philosophy emphasized discipline, strategy, and teamwork, shaping the way the game was played and perceived.

Camp was also an outspoken advocate for player safety. His efforts to minimize injuries and fatalities in the sport led

Walter Camp, 1910

to innovations in protective equipment, such as helmets and pads. His work with the Intercollegiate Football Association (IFA) and later with the Rules Committee helped establish crucial safety standards that continue to evolve to this day.

John Heisman, the famed and legendary coach and player for which the Heisman Trophy is awarded in a celebrated ceremony in New York City, said of Camp:

"I consider him the most important figure that the game of football has developed."

Yet Camp was not without his detractors and his fair share of enemies. A McClure's Magazine story alleged that Camp was in possession of a $100,000 slush fund to use at his discretion. The article also claimed that despite Camp's claims the game was becoming more violent through his changes. The article led then President of the Unite States Theodore Roosevelt to intervene. The result was the creation of the NCAA which made sure to work in Harvard's advantage and against the Yale program of Walter Camp. Teddy Roosevelt was of course a proud graduate of Harvard.

The two colossal leaders did find common ground. Most notably, Camp's vision turned a primitive — and often deadly — college activity into a uniquely American sporting spectacle with passionate devotees at the high school, college and professional levels.

Thirty-seven men were killed on college football fields in the 1904 and 1905 seasons. The national outcry over the brutality forged a partnership between President Theodore Roosevelt and Walter Camp that made football less brutal and more popular than ever.

Theodore Roosevelt, the 26th President of the United States, left an indelible mark on American history through his dynamic leadership, unwavering determination, and robust embodiment of masculinity. A man of multifaceted talents and passions, Roosevelt's life and presidency exemplified a unique blend of physical vigor, intellectual prowess, and moral fortitude that defined his approach to governance and personal conduct.

Born on October 27, 1858, in New York City, Theodore Roosevelt was shaped by a privileged yet challenging upbringing that instilled in him a sense of resilience and fortitude. Afflicted by asthma as a child, he dedicated himself to physical activities such as boxing, hunting, and ranching, which not only bolstered his physical prowess but also fostered a rugged, outdoorsman persona that would become a hallmark of his character.

Roosevelt's toughness and resolve was further solidified during his service as the Assistant Secretary of the Navy and his subsequent participation in the Spanish-American War. He epitomized bravery and fearlessness, leading the Rough Riders—a diverse group of soldiers hailing from various backgrounds—during the Battle of San Juan Hill, a defining moment that showcased his exceptional leadership and valor on the battlefield. Roosevelt would display this bravery, toughness and resolve throughout his life.

On October 14, 1912, Theodore Roosevelt was delivering a campaign speech in Milwaukee when he was shot by a would-be assassin named John Schrank. The bullet struck Roosevelt in the chest, but his thick coat and the folded copy of his speech in his breast pocket helped cushion the impact and potentially saved his life. Despite the injury, Roosevelt remarkably continued his speech, reassuring the crowd that the wound was not severe. His determination to complete his address in the face of such adversity showcased his unwavering commitment to his political ideals and his resolve to persevere amid adversity.

The new sport of football very much appealed to Roosevelt for all the same virtues of courage, bravery, strength, determination and toughness that were exhibited throughout his life. President Theodore Roosevelt, who praised the sport for helping forge a culture of American vitality and masculinity, could no longer fend off the public. "I believe in rough games and in rough, manly sports," the President said in 1903.

As appealing as the game was, it could not continue with dead bodies being carried from the field. It led the President to invite Walter Camp to the White House by letter for those very talks that led to the creation of the NCAA with the goal to avert the fatalities and brutal injuries being witnessed on the field. Many of Camp's very rule changes and suggestions led to the evolution of safety for players participating in the game.

The football talks between Roosevelt and Camp served as a catalyst for significant reforms aimed at prioritizing player safety and minimizing the risk of injuries. Camp, drawing on his deep understanding of the game, proposed a series of rule changes, including the introduction of the forward pass and the implementation of the neutral zone, which contributed to a reduction in dangerous plays and minimized the prevalence of high-impact collisions. Furthermore, the talks laid the foundation for the establishment of standardized safety protocols and equipment requirements, marking a pivotal shift towards a more regulated and secure playing environment for football players at all levels.

In addition to focusing on safety measures, the discussions between Roosevelt and Camp emphasized the importance of fostering sportsmanship and fair play among players and teams. Roosevelt's emphasis on the development of character and integrity through athletic competition aligned with Camp's vision for promoting ethical conduct and camaraderie on the field. Their joint efforts sought to instill a sense of discipline and mutual respect within the realm of football, emphasizing the values of teamwork, perseverance, and respect for one's opponents.

The talks between President Roosevelt and Walter Camp left an indelible mark on the history of American football, laying the groundwork for its evolution into a regulated and more safety-conscious sport. The reforms and regulations implemented as a result of their discussions not only enhanced the overall playing experience for athletes but also contributed to the continued growth and popularity of football across the nation. Moreover, their collective emphasis on sportsmanship and fair play reinforced the significance of character development and ethical conduct in athletic endeavors, leaving a lasting legacy that continues to resonate within the football community.

The football talks between President Theodore Roosevelt and Walter Camp in 1905 served as a pivotal moment in the history of American football, ushering in a new era of safety, regulation, and sportsmanship. Their shared commitment to enhancing player safety and promoting ethical conduct on the field underscored the importance of preserving the integrity of the sport while prioritizing the well-being of its participants. The legacy of their discussions continues to shape the contemporary landscape of American football, highlighting the enduring significance of their contributions to the sport's development and cultural impact.

Camp also left his mark on the sport in other ways than just coaching. Despite being employed full time by the New Haven Clock Company and serving as the volunteer coach and advisor for Yale football, Camp found the time to write. At the time of his death, Camp had written nearly 30 books and over 250 articles appearing in such publications as

Harper's Weekly, Collier's, and Outlook.

Walter was nicknamed the "Father of Football" by Harper's Weekly columnist Caspar Whitney when he was only 33 years old. Most people assume those titles posthumously. Camp lived with the weight of the title throughout his life. It was soon after, that Camp developed what he called an All-American Team- the best players from across the country. Some would argue his team had a severe east coast bias and heavy slant to the Ivy League itself. Yet it became a mainstay for early football fans.

Camp's initiatives were not confined to just the football field. He was a proponent of physical exercise and an innovator in training the body. He became so well known for his efforts that he was approached by both the United States Army and Navy during World War I to help troops develop better physical conditioning. The military brass thought there was no one better to train men to go to war than the man who trained them to battle on the field. He developed a system called The Daily Dozen. A set of 12 exercises completed in repetitive and quick fashion.

Walter Camp died on March 14, 1925, in New York City at the age of 65. His college coaching record was 79 wins, 3 ties and only 5 losses in his entire career at Yale and Stanford combined. He was an innovator and a patriot. A dreamer and a doer.

Camp's contributions to American football did not go unnoticed. In 1951, the Walter Camp Football Foundation was established in his honor, and it continues to present the Walter Camp Player of the Year Award, one of the most prestigious awards in college football. Camp's legacy is also celebrated with the annual Walter Camp All-America Team, recognizing outstanding college football players.

Walter Camp's influence on American football is immeasurable. As The Father of American Football, he not only shaped the game's rules but also instilled principles of teamwork and safety that continue to guide the sport. His innovative thinking and dedication to improving the sport left an enduring legacy that has contributed to the growth and popularity of football in the United States and beyond. Walter Camp's name will forever be synonymous with the sport he helped transform into the gridiron spectacle that captivates millions of fans today.

3 BLOOD, SWEAT & HATE

"Why doesn't Army football have its own website? They couldn't string together 3 W's in a row!"
A Navy Fan's Sign Featured on ESPN's College GameDay 2015

At the root of the passion of college football is truly the axiom of Us vs. Them. In the post-Civil War era it was the opportunity for young men to feel the camaraderie they felt on the battlefield. It became town vs. town and institution vs. institution. Even US Presidents waded into the Us vs. Them as Teddy Roosevelt fought for his Harvard men against the perceived Yale oppressors and Walter Camp.

The truth is that college football would not have survived without the passionate exchange of blood, sweat and hate. Rivalries created passion and energy. It was the reason hundreds and then thousands and then tens of thousands began to surround the field with excitement. To understand the true story of the game it is impossible not to examine the story of significant rivalries that have existed since the early days following the Civil War.

The Harvard-Yale football rivalry, also known as "The Game," is one of the most storied and celebrated college football rivalries in the United States. Dating back to 1875, this enduring contest between two of the nation's oldest and most prestigious universities has captured the hearts of football enthusiasts and alumni for nearly 150 years.

The seeds of the Harvard-Yale football rivalry were planted in the mid-19th century when both universities were at the forefront of American higher education. In 1875, Harvard challenged Yale to a football game, marking the inception of what would become an enduring tradition. The first contest took place on November 13, 1875, and ended in a 4-0 victory for Harvard.

Throughout the late 19th and early 20th centuries, the rivalry intensified, with both teams vying for supremacy on the football field. The competition was marked by a series of closely contested games and iconic moments.

The Harvard-Yale football rivalry transcended the field of play, becoming a symbol of academic and athletic excellence. The game captured the imagination of fans and showcased the dedication and spirit of the players. Moreover, the rivalry evolved in response to changes in football rules and styles, reflecting the broader evolution of American football itself.

The two teams hate each other so much that the school fight songs mention each other by name. The signature Harvard fight song, "Ten Thousand Men of Harvard", names Yale in the famous final stanza. The song is sung in the Harvard football locker room after a victory regardless of the opponent. The song is among six Harvard fight songs that mention Yale. "Down the Field" is Yale's signature fight song and Harvard is the named foe. The song is among five that mention Harvard. Two of the songs, "Bingo, That's the Lingo" and "Goodnight, Harvard", have been sung substituting Princeton for Harvard when appropriate. Cole Porter composed the former and Douglas Moore the latter.

The Harvard-Yale football rivalry continues to captivate audiences today, attracting fans from both universities and beyond. While the game maintains its historical significance, it also serves as a gathering point for alumni, students, and football enthusiasts. The atmosphere at "The Game" is electric, with fans donning school colors and traditions on full display.

The Princeton-Rutgers football rivalry is one of the oldest and most historically significant rivalries in the annals of American college football. Originating in the late 19th century, this enduring contest between two venerable institutions has played a pivotal role in shaping the sport's early history.

The roots of the Princeton-Rutgers rivalry stretch back to the formative years of American football. Both Princeton University and Rutgers University were at the forefront of early collegiate football, contributing significantly to the sport's development. The first recorded meeting between the two teams took place on November 6, 1869, making it one of the earliest intercollegiate football games in history. Rutgers emerged victorious in that inaugural match, winning 6-4.

Several key moments in the rivalry's history have left an indelible mark. The 1882 game, played on a snowy Thanksgiving Day, is particularly memorable. Princeton secured a victory in a thrilling 4-0 match, a result that still reverberates in the annals of the rivalry. The 1930s saw a resurgence in the rivalry, as both teams enjoyed periods of success, keeping the competition fierce and spirited.

Today, the Princeton-Rutgers football rivalry endures as a symbol of historical and sporting significance. Although the frequency of meetings has diminished over the years due to changes in conference affiliations and scheduling, the legacy of these early contests remains strong. The rivalry continues to inspire a sense of tradition and pride, celebrating the rich history of American collegiate football.

The Army-Navy football rivalry, an annual college football contest between the United States Military Academy (Army) and the United States Naval Academy (Navy), is one of the most storied and cherished rivalries in American sports. The rivalry is still a focal point of the college football season today and featured on national television every year. It is traditionally the final regular season football game of the NCAA Division I season played.

John Feinstein in his incredible book, A Civil War: Army vs. Navy- A Year Inside College Football's Purest Rivalry, discussed the background of the famed rivalry:

"The notion of football as war has been used as a metaphor for as long as the game has been played. Coaches see themselves as generals, their assistants as the officers, the players as the soldiers. The violent nature of the sport lends itself easily to the notion that every game is about killing or being killed.

It is logical, then, that the military academies, which train young men- and for the last twenty years, women- to fight wars, would play football with great passion. And once upon a time, when there was a military draft that meant many athletes had to serve in the armed forces, when being a military officer paid as much as or more than a job in the National Football League paid, and when the United States was undefeated in war, truly great and gifted players flocked to West Point to play for Army and to Annapolis to play for Navy."

The origins of the Army-Navy football rivalry date back to November 29, 1890, when the two military academies first faced off on the football field at "The Plain" on the campus at West Point. At the time, football was a burgeoning sport, and these young cadets and midshipmen were eager to establish their dominance. Navy won the inaugural game 24-0, but it was only the beginning of what would become an annual tradition.

Navy Midshipman (and later Admiral) Joseph Mason Reeves wore what is widely regarded as the first football helmet in the 1893 Army–Navy Game. He had been advised by a Navy doctor that another kick to his head would result in intellectual disability or even death, so he commissioned an Annapolis shoemaker to make him a helmet out of leather.

Over the years, the Army-Navy football rivalry has produced numerous iconic moments. In 1913, the rivalry saw its first scoreless tie, a game that still stands as one of the most famous matchups in college football history. The 1945 game, played just days after World War II ended, featured a thrilling Army victory, and both teams carried victory flags symbolizing the ultimate triumph of the Allied forces. In 1963, President John F. Kennedy attended the game and initiated the tradition of awarding the winning team the Commander-in-Chief's Trophy.

The Army-Navy football game draws national attention and is often the culminating event of the college football season. It has been attended by U.S. Presidents, celebrities, and dignitaries. The rivalry has also been showcased in popular culture, including books, films, and documentaries, further cementing its place in American history.

The Alabama-Auburn football rivalry, famously known as the "Iron Bowl," is one of the most intense and storied rivalries in American college football. Rooted in a deep-seated and passionate rivalry between the two universities, this annual contest captures the hearts of fans and defines the football culture of the state of Alabama. If ever a rivalry were described as a mix of blood, sweat and hate it would be the Iron Bowl. The rivalry reflects the political climate during the Reconstruction Period following the Civil War in Alabama, and largely throughout the south.

The game became the extension of a bitter political debate which took place in the Alabama State Legislature regarding the location of the new land-grant college under the state's application under the Morrill Land Grant Act of 1862 during the Civil War Reconstruction Era. The state legislature, influenced by a heavy contingent of representatives who were University of Alabama alumni, pushed to sell the land scripts of 240,000 acres acquired from the Morrill Act or have any new land holdings held in conjunction with the University of Alabama in Tuscaloosa.

The debate lasted over four years, until Lee County and the City of Auburn won the location of the new university in 1872, after donating more than a hundred acres and the remaining buildings and property of the East Alabama Male College. At the time of the Auburn decision the state legislature and governorship were controlled by politicians such as "Scalawag" Southern Republicans and Freedman African-Americans. By 1874, former Confederate and "Redeemer" forces from the Democratic Party gradually overturned the Republican and Freedman control of the Alabama state legislature. The Democrats then attempted to overturn most legislation passed during the Reconstruction Period, including the founding of the new land-grant college at Auburn.

What followed was an intense fight for the survival of Auburn for nearly a decade. Alabama lowered its tuition and academic standards to accept more students. It argued that it had lost years of development due to the Civil War and had not reopened until 1871 when the campus could be rebuilt so it had the right to be aggressive in growth at the cost of the cross-state rival.

Alabama and Auburn played their first football game in Lakeview Park in Birmingham, Alabama, on February 22, 1893. Auburn won 32–22, before an estimated crowd of 5,000. Alabama considered the game to be the final matchup of the 1892 season while Auburn recorded it as the first matchup of 1893.

The Iron Bowl is unique in the world of college football due to its intense and unyielding nature. The deep-rooted passion of Alabama and Auburn fans gives the game a unique atmosphere, with each side proudly displaying their school colors and traditions. Families and communities often find themselves divided, with loyalties running deep.

The rivalry has not only been significant within the state of Alabama but has also held national implications. Both Alabama and Auburn have consistently been among the top programs in college football. The Iron Bowl often serves as a crucial game in determining conference and national championships, making it a must-watch for college football fans nationwide.

The rivalry between the University of Georgia (UGA) Bulldogs and the Georgia Institute of Technology (Georgia Tech) Yellow Jackets is a longstanding and spirited competition that captivates the state of Georgia each year. Known simply as "Clean, Old-Fashioned Hate," this football rivalry is marked by fierce competition, passionate fans, and a rich history dating back over a century.

The roots of the Georgia-Georgia Tech rivalry can be traced back to 1893 when the two teams first clashed on the football field. Georgia Tech won that inaugural matchup 28-6, igniting the rivalry between the state's flagship university

(UGA) and its premier engineering institute (Georgia Tech). The proximity of the two institutions and their desire to establish football supremacy in Georgia set the stage for a historic competition.

The Georgia-Georgia Tech rivalry is deeply embedded in the cultural fabric of the state. It goes beyond the football field, influencing traditions, family loyalties, and social dynamics. Tailgating, colorful chants, and spirited fanfare are integral parts of the rivalry experience, bringing together Georgians of all backgrounds to celebrate their chosen teams.

The Rivalry stories could go on. The University of Southern California vs. Notre Dame. Michigan vs. Ohio State. Texas vs. Oklahoma. Each rivalry has its own place in significance of the development of college football. Each game has its own name. There is no doubt that at the center of the pageantry of college football is an intense love for both tradition and for hating someone traditionally.

4 LEATHERHEADS

"Continued innovation is the best way to beat the competition."
Thomas Edison

 The young midshipman from Annapolis sat nervously in the doctor's office. There was no doubt of his importance for Navy in the upcoming annual rivalry game with Army. The year was 1893 and the cadet was visiting the doctor to discuss head injuries from football. He would not be the last.
 Joseph Mason Reeves was such a ferocious competitor on the football field that he had been nicknamed "Bull" by his teammates. It would be a nickname he would carry for life. Reeves was awaiting the doctor's prognosis this morning and worried he would be limited in football- or worse- the news that he would be forbidden from playing altogether.
 Born on November 20, 1872, in Zanesville, Ohio, Reeves exhibited a strong desire toward military service from an early age. His family's rich military background and his upbringing in a patriotic atmosphere instilled in him a deep sense of duty and commitment to his country. His family's

service in the military could be drawn like a tapestry from the Revolution to the War of 1812 to The Civil War. He knew early on of his desire to one day be one of the midshipmen at the Naval Academy in Annapolis, Maryland.

The doctor entered the room with immediate bad news. He informed the young Reeves that if he were to continue playing football, he risked a fatally traumatic head injury or even what the doctor termed as instant insanity. No, for the young man from Zanesville, Ohio, the doctor's recommendation was that he give up football entirely and focus on his studies.

Joseph "Bull" Reeves left the doctor's office dejected. But only for a minute. Soon a pattern of creatively attacking problems that would define the rest of his life grasped him. He knew what he needed to do.

Reeves made his way through the fish markets and cobbled streets of Annapolis to a well-known shoemaker. The man worked commonly with thick leathers. Reeves asked him to fashion a thick leather moleskin hat with ear guards. It was at this moment that the football helmet was born, and leatherheads began to usher in the true popularity of the sport.

Reeves himself would go on to prominence. After graduation, Reeves was assigned to the cruiser USS *San Francisco*. He served on the battleship USS *Oregon* during the Spanish–American War, taking part in the action against Admiral Pascual Cervera y Topete's fleet at Santiago de Cuba in June and July 1898.

Reeves' career witnessed a significant turning point during World War I when he was appointed as the commander of a battleship squadron in the Atlantic Fleet. His exceptional leadership during this period earned him widespread recognition and respect among his peers. Reeves's innovative tactics and decisive decision-making

Admiral Joseph "Bull" Reeves

skills played a crucial role in safeguarding the fleet and securing vital sea routes, contributing significantly to the Allied victory in the war.

Admiral Joseph Reeves would revisit his leather helmet once more. There was considerable concern about the new usage of aircraft and paratroopers jumping out of those aircraft as the military considered new forms of warfare. One of the problems in training was the continued head injuries of those paratroopers. Reeves suggested his leather helmet. The military adopted it.

Reeves would go on to serve through World War II. He also coached Navy football. Of all his football accomplishments he would say that having a 6-0 record against Army was the greatest.

The leather helmet soon began to sweep the country. In the early days of American football, players like Reeves participated without any head protection, exposing themselves to the inherent risks associated with the physical nature of the game. However, as concerns about player safety grew, the introduction of the leather football helmet in the early 20th century represented a significant step forward in protecting players from potential head injuries.

The leather helmet's design featured a basic, yet innovative, approach to safeguarding players. It comprised a hard, yet pliable, leather exterior, often reinforced with padding and sometimes a crude suspension system to absorb impacts. The helmet's construction aimed to mitigate the risks of head trauma, concussions, fatalities and other injuries commonly associated with the rough-and-tumble nature of early football.

Throughout the 1910s and 1920s, the leather football helmet underwent several modifications and improvements to enhance its protective capabilities. Manufacturers experimented with different padding materials, refined the shape and fit, and incorporated additional reinforcement in critical areas. As the sport gained popularity and the understanding of head injuries deepened, the helmet's design continued to evolve, setting the stage for more advanced forms of head protection in the years to come.

Next to the pigskin itself, no piece of equipment is more synonymous with American football than the helmet. Initially an outlier, over the past nearly 130 years it has transitioned from elective to essential, from rudimentary to high-tech and from utilitarian to branding mainstay.

Because it cradles the head of each participant, the football helmet is regarded as the key piece of gear in making the sport safer to play. For that reason, advancements and innovations in headgear are being announced with increasing frequency. Yet, as has been proven throughout the sport's history, rules and equipment are only part of the ultimate equation.

While the leather football helmet played a pivotal role in enhancing player safety during its era, its limitations became increasingly apparent with the advancement of the game and the recognition of the long-term risks associated with repetitive head trauma. As a result, the development of more sophisticated and technologically advanced helmets gained momentum, eventually leading to the introduction of modern, high-impact-resistant helmets made from materials like polycarbonate and other composite materials.

Despite its eventual displacement by more advanced headgear, the leather football helmet remains an iconic symbol of the sport's rich history and evolution. It serves as a testament to the enduring commitment of athletes, coaches, and sporting authorities to prioritize player safety and well-being, highlighting the continuous efforts to improve protective equipment in response to the evolving challenges of the game.

It was during this time in the 1910s that college football really began to explode in popularity. Those leather helmet wearing players became known as Leatherheads. Everyone had their favorite player to watch. From the rapid growth of collegiate athletic programs to the emergence of legendary coaches and players, the decade left an indelible mark on the history and development of college football.

One innovation from the early 1900s period was hardened leather. In 1917, the first helmets were raised above the head in an attempt to direct blows away from the top of the head. Ear flaps also had their downfall during this period as they had little ventilation and made it difficult for players to hear. The 1920s marked the first time that helmets were used by the majority in the sport of football. These helmets were made of leather and had some padding on the inside, but the padding was insufficient and provided little protection. In addition, they lacked face masks. As a result, injuries were very common. Early helmets also absorbed a lot of heat, making them very uncomfortable to wear.

At the beginning of the 1910s, college football had already gained substantial popularity across the nation. Spectators flocked to stadiums to witness thrilling matchups between rival teams, fostering a sense of school pride and community spirit. The sport served as a rallying point for universities, attracting enthusiastic fans and fostering strong alumni connections, thereby solidifying its position as an integral part of American collegiate culture.

The 1910s were characterized by a remarkable surge in the competitiveness and intensity of college football. As the sport gained more recognition, universities invested heavily in developing robust athletic programs, hiring renowned coaches and recruiting exceptional players. Teams focused on implementing innovative strategies and refining their gameplay, leading to a surge in the overall standard of play and the evolution of various tactical approaches.

The period also witnessed the emergence of legendary figures who would shape the future of college football. Influential coaches such as Pop Warner, Knute Rockne, and Fielding H. Yost pioneered new coaching techniques and introduced innovative offensive and defensive strategies that transformed the dynamics of the game. Their coaching philosophies emphasized discipline, strategic planning, and teamwork, setting the standards for excellence and sportsmanship that continue to define college football to this day.

Seeking to make the sport still safer, in 1939 college rules made the helmet mandatory and the NFL followed suit four years later. Meanwhile, John T. Riddell was developing the first plastic helmet, featuring an inner liner suspension system that absorbed and better distributed the impact. Not only did NFL teams take notice, so did the U.S. military, which, upon with the endorsement of Major General George Patton, modified it for widespread use by the Army during World War II. Schutt became the first to manufacture facemasks.

Chin straps were soon added, and by 1949, the plastic model was omnipresent, both among pros and amateurs. One time art student and Los Angeles Rams halfback Fred Gehrke started a branding revolution, painting ram horns on an old college helmet. Rams management loved it and commissioned Gehrke to paint all the team's headgear. Upon seeing the branded helmets for the first time, a stadium full of Rams fans erupted in a lengthy standing ovation. Continuing throughout the Fifties, virtually every team in America conducted a helmet makeover, adding distinctive colors or an emblem and baking them into plastic.

There is no headgear, however, quite as romantic to the history and imagery of football as the leatherhead. There was one leatherhead who was more renowned than any other in the country. In a nation that celebrates larger than life heroes- he was the largest the game had known to this point. He would go on to be a hall of fame football player, professional baseball player, NCAA champion, Olympic decathlon champion and ballroom dancing champion. There seemed to be nothing that James Francis Thorpe could not do.

5 JIM THORPE

"I played football because I loved it. I didn't play for money or fame; I played for the thrill of the game."
Jim Thorpe

Coach Glenn Scobey Warner, affectionately known as Pop, was filled with anticipation that Fall day. To say that football was his life would be fair. He played at Cornell and had helped develop new techniques such as the 3-point stance. Warner had previously coached at Iowa State, Georgia and his alma-mater Cornell. Now he was heading the program at Carlisle Indian Industrial School in Carlisle, Pennsylvania.

Born on April 5, 1871, in Springville, New York, Warner exhibited an early affinity for athletics, particularly football. His journey into coaching began at the University of Georgia in 1895, where he served as the head coach for one season. Following this, he moved on to Cornell University, leading the team to an impressive 33-game winning streak, an achievement that marked the commencement of a long and illustrious career.

Pop Warner's true legacy lies in his innovative approach to the game. He was among the first to emphasize the importance of strategy and technique, advocating for a more cerebral approach to football. Warner's coaching style focused on agility, discipline, and precision, revolutionizing the training methodologies of his time. His contributions to the evolution of the forward pass, the single- and double-wing formations, and the implementation of the screen pass, among other strategies, changed the landscape of American football.

Beyond his coaching prowess, Pop Warner's vision extended to the educational development of young athletes. In 1929, he founded the Pop Warner Little Scholars program, aiming to instill fundamental values such as sportsmanship, teamwork, and academic excellence in youth athletes. The program has since become a cornerstone of youth football in the United States, emphasizing the importance of both athletic prowess and academic achievement. He had no idea that today would be a special day that would go on to be the formation of such a legendary career.

Coach Pop Warner Overseeing Jim Thorpe

Carlisle was once a prominent football school celebrating two national championships at the end of the 19th Century. So desperate to return to prominence the school offered the acclaimed Pop Warner a salary of $1,200 ($42,000 today) to coach football. It was the highest salary anyone had ever been paid to coach the new game. Warner knew success was key.

So today was a day to be excited. The Carlilse team needed desperate help in the way of talent and Warner believed that talent would be coming to the try out in a young man named Jim Thorpe.

The myth surrounding Jim Thorpe is difficult to separate from the truth because so many witnessed his accomplishments that otherwise would have seemed impossible. In 1907, Thorpe was walking past the campus when he saw the school's track and field team practicing. He had never tried the high jump before but thought he could do better than anyone there. Without changing from his street clothes, Jim Thorpe recorded a school record of 5 feet 9 inches in the high jump on his first ever attempt.

A legend was born.

Thorpe's parents were both of mixed-race ancestry and he battled prejudice as a young man. His father, Hiram Thorpe, had an Irish father and a Sac and Fox Indian mother. His mother, Charlotte Vieux, had a French father and a Potawatomi mother, a descendant of Chief Louis Vieux. Thorpe was raised as a Sac and Fox, and his native name, *Wa-Tho-Huk*, is translated as "path lit by great flash of lightning" or, more simply, "Bright Path." As was the custom for Sac and Fox, he was named for something occurring around the time of his birth, in this case the light brightening the path to the cabin where he was born. Thorpe's parents were both Roman Catholic, a faith which Thorpe observed throughout his adult life.

Thorpe attended the Sac and Fox Indian Agency school in Stroud, with his twin brother, Charlie. Charlie helped him through school until he died of pneumonia when they were nine years old. Thorpe ran away from school several times. His father sent him to the Haskell Institute, an Indian boarding school in Lawrence, Kansas, so that he would not run away again.

Thorpe's mother soon died during childbirth complications. It devastated the young man. After a grueling time of battling his father, he agreed to attend school at Carlisle Indian Industrial School. It would be the decision that would alter the course of his life.

This day Pop waited to see the campus star in action. Thorpe was valuable to the school. He would soon compete in the Olympics representing the school on the world stage. He was a champion in baseball, lacrosse and ballroom dancing. The school was concerned he might be injured playing football. Warner thought he might be just the star he needed, and football might be the destiny that Thorpe needed.

Warner had worked with his returners on defense for weeks and knew it would be the strong unit of his team. He decided to try Thorpe at running back. On the first play, Warner would later write that the 6'1" 202lbs giant of a man "ran around, past and through them not once, but twice." He went on to add that Thorpe walked towards him and flipped him the ball while saying, "Nobody is going to tackle Jim."

Thorpe's journey to national and global athletic stardom began that day and during his time at the Carlisle Indian Industrial School in Pennsylvania. Under the mentorship of renowned coach "Pop" Warner, Thorpe honed his natural athletic abilities and showcased exceptional talent in various sports, including football, where he gained nationwide recognition for his exceptional skills as a running back, kicker, and defensive player.

Carlisle Indian Industrial School returned to prominence. The team finished 11-1 in 1912. Carlisle won the national collegiate championship in large part due to the addition of Thorpe. He scored 25 Touchdowns during the season. He rushed 191 times for 1,869 yards. It should also be noted that the statistics of 2 games that season have been lost. His actual tally was much higher.

The team defeated powerhouses Army and Harvard. The Army game was especially memorable. At one point of the game Thorpe appeared to score on a 92-yard touchdown. The play was called back due to holding. In the huddle, Thorpe requested the same play be called again. This time he ran for a 97-yard touchdown. A young Army cadet playing against Thorpe in the that game named Dwight D. Eisenhower would later say:

"Here and there, there are some people who are supremely endowed. My memory goes back to Jim Thorpe. He never practiced in his life, and he could do anything better than any other football player I ever saw."

In 1912, at the Stockholm Olympics, Jim Thorpe's remarkable versatility and athleticism were brought to the world stage. Despite minimal training, he achieved unprecedented success, securing gold medals in both the pentathlon and decathlon events. Thorpe's triumph at the Olympics solidified his status as one of the greatest athletes of his time, earning him global acclaim and admiration for his unparalleled feats of strength, speed, and agility.

Following his Olympic triumph, Thorpe transitioned to professional football and baseball, showcasing his exceptional talent in both sports. He played professional football for teams such as the Canton Bulldogs, the Cleveland Indians, and the New York Giants, earning a reputation as a dominant force on the field. His contributions to the early development of professional football were instrumental in popularizing the sport and establishing its place in American culture.

Beyond football, Thorpe's foray into professional baseball highlighted his exceptional skills as a player and solidified his reputation as a versatile and multifaceted athlete. His remarkable achievements in both football and baseball underscored his exceptional abilities that cemented his legacy as one of the most celebrated athletes of his generation.

Thorpe was the original multi-sport star before anyone had ever dreamed of Bo Jackson or Deion Sanders. Biographer Ron Flatter wrote the following of Thorpe's impact and Olympic exploits:

"We certainly never saw him in person. But we sure knew the legend. He was the Olympic track champion who lost his gold medals because he played minor league baseball. Long before Bo and Deion, he was the athlete who played pro baseball and football at the same time.

He was voted "The Greatest Athlete of the First Half of the Century" by the Associated Press and became a charter member of the Pro Football Hall of Fame. But Thorpe's legend was galvanized into America's conscience at the 1912 Olympics.

He won the decathlon and pentathlon in Stockholm. When King Gustav V of Sweden congratulated Thorpe, he said, "Sir, you are the greatest athlete in the world."

Thorpe reputedly replied only, "Thanks, king."

The idea of the sports hero in America was born. Spectators would travel far and wide to catch a glimpse of Thorpe. He even eventually sold the rights of his life as a film for $15,000.

Despite the accolades and widespread admiration, Thorpe faced numerous challenges and controversies throughout his career, including the revocation of his Olympic titles due to his brief stint as a semi-professional baseball player, an issue that remains a subject of debate and contention in the history of sports.

He struggled in his post-athletic career. Known as a generous man, Thorpe was often taken advantage of and fleeced of what little money his career had garnered him. Thorpe was not blessed to have been an athlete in today's culture of large contracts.

He worked as a construction worker, stuntman, actor, bouncer, security guard and ditchdigger. As glorious as the 1910s had been for Thorpe, the late 1920s and 1930s became a nightmare. There seemed to be one opponent he could not beat. The Great Depression took an incredible toll on Thorpe. He lost his job, his house and what seemed to be his notoriety. He turned to drinking and by the early 1950s was penniless when he died.

Jim Thorpe was not the only one challenged by The Great Depression. It was about to take its aim at all of College Football.

6 SOMETHING TO PLAY FOR

"It is ridiculous for a country to get all worked up about a game— except the Super Bowl, of course. Now that's important."
Andy Rooney

Millions of people would crowd around the television set to hear the Roopville, Georgia, native introduce the game. Roopville, Georgia, is located on the Georgia and Alabama state lines in Carroll County. The fact that the small town boasts a population of only 200 never stopped the boy from dreaming.

Keith Jackson, a name synonymous with the passion and thrill of college football, was a trailblazing sportscaster whose warm voice and charismatic presence left an indelible mark on the landscape of sports commentary. Born on October 18, 1928, in Roopville, Georgia, Jackson embarked on a remarkable journey that transformed him into an icon of sports journalism, revered for his unparalleled ability to capture the essence of sporting events and convey the passion of the moment to audiences across the nation.

Jackson's early life was characterized by an affinity for

sports, an inclination that would eventually pave the way for his illustrious career. After attending Washington State University, he delved into the world of broadcasting, initially working as a news reporter before transitioning into sports journalism. His natural talent and unwavering dedication soon propelled him into the limelight, leading to his first notable role as a radio broadcaster for the Washington Huskies.

Throughout his career, Keith Jackson became synonymous with some of the most iconic moments in sports history. His resonant voice narrated numerous defining moments in college football, including the famed Rose Bowl games and the annual spectacle of the NCAA Football Championships. Jackson's distinctive style, marked by his folksy expressions and vivid storytelling, endeared him to millions of viewers, establishing a deep emotional connection between the audience and the events unfolding on the field.

Jackson's expressions were well known throughout the tapestry of college football. "Whoa Nellie!" "Fum-BLE!" "Hold the phonnnne!" All these expressions made their mark and led to Jackson becoming one of the most famous college football voices. It was one expression however that was coined by Jackson that brilliantly captured the history of the game.

"The Grandaddy of them all!"

For nearly two decades millions would scoot closer to their television to hear Keith Jackson's famed introduction to the Rose Bowl. He couldn't have been more accurate. Founded in 1902, The Rose Bowl truly was the grandaddy of them all.

The game was originally called the "Tournament East-West Football Game with the first meeting taking place on January 1, 1902. It was the first of what would become known as New Year's Day Bowl Games. The game was originally conceived to help pay for the struggling Rose Parade in Pasadena, California.

The first game featured the impressive University of Michigan representing the East and Stanford University representing the West. The Michigan coach added to the spice of the day. Fielding H. Yost had previously walked the sidelines at Stanford during the prior year. Now he was a Michigan man. The local papers ensured a great spectacle of football.

The game was a disaster for the organizers from the onset. Michigan crushed Stanford by a score of 49-0 and Stanford actually quit in the third quarter. The Michigan team that would go on to finish 11-0 and win the National Championship was just too much for the Stanford Cardinal. To say that the pride of the Cardinal was blemished would be an understatement. The crowd was left bewildered and confused at the game they had come to witness. Many requested refunds for the game that did not finish.

The pain was so great that the Tournament of Roses board tried various other spectacles for the next thirteen years before giving the Rose Bowl a chance again in 1916. They tried chariot races, ostrich races, boxing matches and more before finally going back to football. But, on New Year's Day in 1916 the football bowl game returned for good as the State College of Washington (now Washington State University) defeated Brown University in the first of what was to become the annual tradition featuring the champion of the Big Ten verse the champion of the Pac 10 until the initiation of the College Football Playoff system.

Before the Rose Bowl was built, games were played in Pasadena's Tournament Park, approximately three miles southeast of the current Rose Bowl stadium, near the campus of Caltech. Tournament Park was found to be unsuitable for the increasingly large crowds gathering to watch the game and a new, permanent home for the game was commissioned.

The Rose Bowl stadium, designed after the Yale Bowl in New Haven, hosted its first "Rose Bowl" game on January 1, 1923. The name of the stadium was alternatively "Tournament of Roses Stadium" or "Tournament of Roses Bowl", until the name "Rose Bowl" was settled on before the 1923 game.

The stadium seating has been reconfigured several times since its original construction in 1922. For many years, the Rose Bowl stadium had the largest football stadium capacity in the United States, eventually being surpassed by Michigan Stadium in 1998. The maximum stated seating capacity was 104,594 from 1972 to 1997. Capacity was lowered after the 1998 game; the 2006 game, which was also the BCS championship game, attracted a crowd of 93,986; and there were 94,118 spectators at the 2011 game between TCU and Wisconsin. As of 2012, the Rose Bowl is number seven on the list of American football stadiums by capacity with a current official seating capacity of 92,542 and is still the largest stadium that hosts post-season bowl games.

The Grandaddy of Them All quickly gave birth to other successful bowl games. In the early 20th century, the concept of postseason bowl games gradually gained traction, providing an opportunity for the best college football teams to showcase their skills and compete in high-stakes matchups following the regular season. Over the decades, numerous bowl games emerged, each with its own distinct traditions and legacies, contributing to the rich tapestry of college football history.

One of the pivotal moments in the evolution of college bowl games was the establishment of the Orange Bowl in 1935, followed by the Sugar Bowl and the Sun Bowl in the late 1930s. These games not only provided a platform for showcasing athletic prowess but also fostered a sense of community and camaraderie among fans, players, and institutions.

The expansion of television in the mid-20th century further accelerated the popularity of college bowl games, allowing audiences across the country to witness the excitement and drama unfold in real time. The Rose Bowl, Orange Bowl, Sugar Bowl, and Cotton Bowl, among others, became annual spectacles that captivated millions of viewers, solidifying their status as premier events in the American sports calendar.

Perhaps no other bowl stands with as much history as the Sugar Bowl. The Sugar Bowl, one of the most celebrated annual college football bowl games in the United States, has a rich and storied history that reflects the evolution of the sport and its deep-rooted cultural significance. Since its inception in the early 20th century, the Sugar Bowl has become an iconic event that embodies the spirit of competition, camaraderie, and athletic excellence, capturing the hearts of fans and shaping the landscape of college football.

The origins of the Sugar Bowl date back to the 1930s, when the game was first played on January 1, 1935, as part of the New Orleans Mid-Winter Sports Association's efforts to bring a prominent football event to the South. It quickly established itself as a prestigious postseason game, attracting top-tier college football teams from across the country. Over the years, the Sugar Bowl has become synonymous with thrilling matchups, showcasing some of the most memorable moments in the history of the sport.

Throughout the mid-20th century, the Sugar Bowl solidified its reputation as a premier college football event, hosting legendary teams and players who left an indelible mark on the game. Notable matchups and standout performances added to the game's allure, making it a staple in American sports culture. The pageantry, excitement, and fierce competition associated with the Sugar Bowl elevated it to the status of a cherished tradition, eagerly anticipated by fans and players alike.

Furthermore, the Sugar Bowl's significance extends beyond the field, as it has served as a platform for cultural exchange and community engagement. The game's location in New Orleans, renowned for its vibrant culture and festive atmosphere, has provided an exceptional backdrop for celebrating the spirit of college football. The city's unique blend of music, cuisine, and hospitality has enhanced the overall experience for attendees, creating a festive atmosphere that extends well beyond the stadium.

In addition to its cultural impact, the Sugar Bowl has played a pivotal role in shaping the landscape of college football. Through its historical matchups and pivotal games, the Sugar Bowl has contributed to the development of rivalries, the rise of prominent football programs, and the emergence of future professional athletes. The game's influence on the college football playoff system and its role in determining national championships have cemented its place as a cornerstone of the collegiate sports calendar.

As the Sugar Bowl continues to thrive in the modern era, its legacy remains firmly rooted in its commitment to excellence, sportsmanship, and the celebration of the collegiate athletic spirit. The game's enduring tradition of showcasing top-tier teams and delivering unforgettable moments has solidified its status as an integral part of American sports history.

In the following decades, the number of bowl games continued to grow, with new games introduced to accommodate the increasing demand for postseason college football. The Fiesta Bowl, the Peach Bowl, and the Citrus Bowl, among others, emerged as prominent fixtures in the postseason landscape, providing a platform for teams to compete on a national stage and leaving an indelible mark on the history of college football.

The modern era of college bowl games is characterized by an extensive network of matchups, featuring teams from various conferences and regions competing in a diverse array of games. The significance of these bowl games extends beyond the realm of sports, fostering a sense of tradition, pride, and excitement among alumni, students, and communities associated with the participating universities.

In 2022, there were 43 College Football Bowl Games. Most games have conference affiliations. 43 bowl games mean a remarkable number of 86 teams in NCAA Division 1 football receive the opportunity to play in a bowl. There were only 133 teams in Division 1. It is impossible not to wonder what the Grandaddy would have thought about that- or at least Keith Jackson. Whoa Nellie.

7 KNUTE ROCKNE, ALL AMERICAN

"I don't like to lose, and that isn't so much because it is just a football game, but because defeat means the failure to reach your objective."
Knute Rockne

The Norwegian wagonmaker and his wife knew they wanted more for their family than what their current economic reality afforded them. Lars Knutson Rockne and his wife, Marth Pedersdatter Gjermo, decided to take the advice of a cousin who had recently moved to a city called Chicago in the United States. They saved for transportation and boarded their steamer as a family, including their five-year old son. Little did they know that their son Knute would revolutionize the game of football and become one of the greatest celebrities and tragedies in America's history.

Knute Rockne grew up in the Logan Square area of Chicago. He loved everything about his new home. He joined up with a group of boys called the Logan Square Tigers to play football at every chance he had. He played end for the team and many of the boys stayed together playing all the way through their high school graduation at North West Division High School in Chicago.

Rockne knew there was one thing and one thing only that he wanted to do- play football. After his high school graduation, he took a job as a mail dispatcher with the post office for four years. He used those four years to save up enough money to continue his education and play college football. He attended Notre Dame in Indiana to finish his schooling. What transpired from that moment would put Notre Dame on the map of permanent College Football prestige and begin the legacy of Knute Rockne, All American in one unforgettable game.

On November 1, 1913, a historic gridiron showdown unfolded at West Point, New York, between the University of Notre Dame Fighting Irish and the United States Military Academy's Army Black Knights. This football game, a pivotal moment in the early history of both teams, would go on to be remembered as a defining clash that shaped the trajectory of collegiate football in America.

The matchup garnered nationwide attention, drawing a crowd of fervent supporters from across the country. Anticipation was high as both teams entered the field, with Notre Dame seeking to solidify its emerging reputation as a formidable football program, while Army aimed to maintain its dominance within the collegiate sports arena.

The game itself was a display of sheer grit and determination, with both teams fiercely battling for every yard. Notre Dame, led by the indomitable coach Jesse Harper, had cultivated a reputation for its unyielding spirit and innovative tactics. On the other side, Army, under the guidance of the esteemed head coach Charles Dudley Daly, showcased a disciplined and resilient style of play that had earned them widespread acclaim.

The clash between the two powerhouses proved to be a gripping spectacle, with each team showcasing their prowess and tactical ingenuity. Notre Dame's offense, led by the dynamic backfield duo of Gus Dorais and Knute Rockne, demonstrated an unprecedented passing strategy that left the Army defense struggling to counter their innovative aerial assault. The game saw a series of exhilarating plays, with Notre Dame's strategic passing game leading to several decisive touchdowns, establishing a lead that Army found challenging to overcome.

Despite a valiant effort by the Army Black Knights, the Notre Dame Fighting Irish emerged victorious with a resounding 35-13 triumph, solidifying their status as a rising force in the realm of collegiate football. The game's impact reverberated far beyond the final whistle, sparking conversations about the evolution of football strategies and the significance of tactical innovation in the sport.

The Notre Dame-Army clash of November 1913 left an enduring mark on the landscape of American collegiate football, serving as a catalyst for the adoption of advanced passing tactics and strategic gameplay in the years to come. The game's legacy persists as a testament to the resilience, sportsmanship, and unwavering determination that define the spirit of collegiate athletics.

Rockne's fame soared after that game. While the game was not the invention of the forward pass it was the first widely accepted example of successfully impacting a game's outcome. The game also served to cement a national fanbase for Notre Dame. Rockne's impact to college football would not be limited to just his sensational career as a player.

Rockne's impact on the world of football is immeasurable. As a player for the University of Notre Dame, he exhibited exceptional talent and dedication, setting the stage for his illustrious coaching career. It was during his tenure as the head coach at Notre Dame, spanning from 1918 to 1930, that Rockne truly left an indelible mark on the sport. His head coaching record was 105 wins, 12 losses and 5 ties. He revolutionized the game, introducing innovative strategies and fostering a culture of teamwork and discipline that transformed Notre Dame into a football powerhouse. Rockne's emphasis on precision and strategic planning laid the foundation for modern coaching techniques, influencing the evolution of football tactics for decades to come.

Beyond his tactical brilliance, Rockne's coaching philosophy was grounded in instilling values of sportsmanship, integrity, and resilience in his players. His famous "Win one for the Gipper" speech remains an iconic moment in sports history, encapsulating his ability to inspire his team to achieve greatness through unity and determination. Rockne's approach to coaching went beyond the gridiron, shaping the character and values of his players, many of whom went on to become influential figures in their respective fields.

Rockne's legacy extends far beyond the confines of the football field. His impact on popular culture and the collective American consciousness remains palpable. His name became synonymous with excellence and integrity, serving as a beacon of hope and inspiration during a time of social and economic upheaval. Rockne's spirit of resilience and perseverance in the face of adversity continues to inspire individuals from all walks of life, resonating with those who strive for success against all odds.

Rockne was the original walking sports quote. "Show me a good and gracious loser and I'll show you a failure." "Drink the first. Sip the second. Skip the third." "I have found that coaching prayers work best when you have big players." Rockne was beloved in popular culture.

Knute Rockne

His place in the hearts of American fans, as has often been the case in sports, politics and pop culture, was cemented even further by his youthful and untimely death. Rockne died in the crash of a Transcontinental & Western Air airliner in Kansas on March 31, 1931, while on his way to serve as an aid on the production of the film *The Spirit of Notre Dame* (released October 13, 1931). The plane had stopped in Kansas City so that Rockne could visit his sons who were in school there. An hour after taking off from Kansas City, one of the Fokker Trimotor's wings broke up in flight. The plane crashed into a wheat field near Bazaar, Kansas, killing Rockne and everyone else on the plane.

A memorial dedicated to the victims of the plane crash was erected at the spot where the plane crashed. The memorial is surrounded by a wire fence with wooden posts and was maintained for many years by James Heathman, who, at the age of 13 in 1931, was one of the first people to arrive at the site of the crash.

Rockne's shocking death startled the nation and triggered a national outpouring of grief, comparable to the deaths of presidents. President Herbert Hoover called Rockne's death "a national loss". King Haakon VII of Norway knighted Rockne and sent a representative to Rockne's funeral in Chicago.

Rockne was buried in Highland Cemetery in South Bend, the city adjacent to the Notre Dame campus. Six of his current players were selected to carry the coffin (Marty Brill, Tom Yarr, Frank Carideo, Marchy Schwartz, Tom Conley and Larry Mullins). It is estimated that 100,000 people lined the route of his funeral procession, and the funeral, held at the Basilica of the Sacred Heart, was broadcast live on network radio across the United States.

Driven by the public emotion for Rockne and anger of the accident, the crash story played out at length in nearly all the nation's newspapers. The public demanded answers and changes. An investigation into the damage at the accident found it to be that the plane's plywood outer skin was bonded to the ribs and spars with water-based aliphatic resin glue, and flight in rain had caused the bond to deteriorate to the point that sections of the plywood suddenly separated. The national outcry over the disaster triggered changes to aircraft design, manufacturing, operation, inspection, maintenance, regulation and crash investigation, igniting a safety revolution that ultimately transformed airline travel worldwide from one of the most dangerous forms of travel to one of the safest.

The public's fascination with Knute Rockne was nowhere near over. In 1940, the silver screen witnessed the release of a biographical drama that would forever etch itself into the collective consciousness of sports enthusiasts and moviegoers alike. "Knute Rockne, All American," directed by Lloyd Bacon and starring the illustrious actor Pat O'Brien in the titular role, brought to life the extraordinary journey of the legendary football coach Knute Rockne, leaving an indelible mark on the history of sports cinema.

The film chronicles Rockne's path from his humble beginnings as an immigrant to the United States to his rise as a trailblazing figure in the world of American football. O'Brien's powerful portrayal of Rockne captivated audiences, capturing the essence of the coach's unwavering determination, visionary leadership, and profound impact on the game. The film delves into the pivotal moments of Rockne's career, depicting his tenure at the University of Notre Dame and the transformation of the Fighting Irish into a powerhouse of collegiate football.

Central to the film's narrative is the iconic portrayal of Rockne's heartfelt and inspiring speeches, including the renowned "Win one for the Gipper" address, delivered in homage to the late former player George Gipp (played by a young actor named Ronald Reagan). This scene, now etched in the annals of cinematic history, remains an enduring symbol of Rockne's ability to motivate and galvanize his team to achieve greatness, transcending the realms of sports and touching the hearts of audiences worldwide.

Beyond its captivating portrayal of Rockne's life and career, "Knute Rockne, All American" serves as a poignant exploration of the values of resilience, sportsmanship, and the relentless pursuit of excellence. The film resonates with viewers on a deeper level, emphasizing the importance of integrity, teamwork, and the enduring spirit of the human endeavor. Rockne's character, as depicted in the film, embodies the essence of leadership, inspiring individuals to strive for greatness and embrace the challenges that life presents.

"Knute Rockne, All American" remains a timeless testament to the transformative power of sports, showcasing the profound impact of one individual's dedication and vision on the trajectory of an entire team and community. The film's enduring legacy lies in its ability to transcend the boundaries of time, continuing to inspire audiences with its powerful message of determination, perseverance, and the pursuit of excellence.

On March 10, 1988, the town of Rockne, Texas, which was named for Knute in 1931 following his plane crash opened their post office doors with a new 22 cent stamp in honor of Knute Rockne. Across the country the stamps sold out quickly nearly 6 decades after his plane crash. Then former actor turned US President, Ronald Reagan, gave the address at The Athletic & Convocation Center at the University of Notre Dame on March 9, 1988, and officially unveiled the Rockne stamp.

Knute Rockne's life and impact on American football and

society at large remain a testament to the enduring power of determination and leadership. His innovative coaching techniques, unwavering commitment to excellence, and profound influence on the values of sportsmanship continue to inspire athletes and coaches across the globe. Rockne's remarkable journey from a humble beginning to becoming an iconic figure serves as a timeless reminder that through dedication and perseverance, one can transcend boundaries and leave an indelible mark on the world.

8 THE GAME SURVIVES

"The Greatest Generation came of age in The Great Depression, when everyday life was about deprivation and sacrifice, when the economic conditions of the time were so grave and so unrelenting it would have been easy enough for the American dream to fade away."
Tom Brokaw

The 1920s had been good for the game of college football. Rivalries had continued. Crowds had increased. Star players were promoted. Much like the feeling of the rest of the country, the game was growing and there seemed to be nothing that could stop it.

Americans danced the Foxtrot and the Charleston. They discovered Jazz Music for the first time. The automobile was prevalent. The decade saw automobile ownership rise from 8 million in 1920 to 23 million by the end of the decade. The world had survived The Great War. There seemingly was nothing that could stop America.

Then came Monday, October 28, 1929. The Dow lost 13

percent of its market value. On Tuesday it was worse. Another 12 percent was lost. By mid-November the Dow had lost nearly half of its value. The slide continued through the summer of 1932, when the Dow closed at 41.22, its lowest value of the twentieth century, 89 percent below its peak. The Dow did not return to its pre-crash heights until November 1954.

The Great Depression that defined the 1930s impacted nearly every American life and all aspects of everyday life. People lost their jobs at the highest rate in American history. Families lost their savings, homes, farms and businesses. Some families were forced to separate with fathers traveling in attempts to find any nomadic work available. Starvation and poverty gripped the country.

Among the institutions of American life deeply impacted was college football, a sport that had garnered a fervent following across the nation just a decade earlier. As the economic crisis plunged the country into despair, college football faced a myriad of struggles, ranging from financial constraints to dwindling attendance.

During the Great Depression, the financial landscape was bleak, and colleges faced severe budget cuts. Athletics programs were among the first to be affected, with reduced funding leading to slashed budgets and strained resources. College football programs, reliant on funding for travel, equipment, and staff salaries, grappled with the challenge of sustaining themselves. Many colleges were forced to cut back on their football programs, and some were even compelled to suspend their programs temporarily.

The economic hardships experienced by the public also had a significant impact on attendance at college football games. With unemployment rates soaring and families struggling to make ends meet, spending on leisure activities, including attending football games, was perceived as a luxury many simply could not afford. As a result, stadiums that were once filled now saw dwindling crowds, with the atmosphere of excitement and enthusiasm dampened by the prevailing economic gloom.

Despite these challenges, the resilience of college football during the Great Depression was evident through various measures adopted to adapt to the harsh economic climate. College teams began to explore creative ways to cut costs, such as arranging local games to minimize travel expenses. They also sought alternative revenue streams by organizing charity games and events, demonstrating a commitment to supporting their communities in times of need.

Furthermore, college football served as a source of unity and distraction during the hardships of the Great Depression. The sport provided an avenue for communities to come together, rallying behind their teams and finding solace in the competitive spirit and camaraderie fostered by the game. College football continued to inspire hope and resilience, offering a temporary escape from the grim realities of everyday life and instilling a sense of pride and identity within communities struggling to find their footing amidst economic chaos.

Heroes of college football began to emerge from the ashes of depressed society. Perhaps no student athlete gripped the late 1930s as Nile Kinnick. A legendary figure in the annals of American sports, Kinnick, remains an enduring symbol of athletic prowess, academic excellence, and unwavering integrity. Born on July 9, 1918, in Adel, Iowa, Kinnick's impact on the world of football and beyond endures to this day. Renowned for his exceptional football ability, his remarkable academic achievements, and his profound sense of integrity, Kinnick's legacy serves as a beacon of inspiration for generations of athletes and individuals alike.

Kinnick's journey to prominence began during his time at the University of Iowa, where he achieved remarkable feats both on and off the football field. As a member of the Iowa Hawkeyes football team, Kinnick's athletic prowess was unparalleled. His remarkable talent as a halfback and his exceptional abilities as a kick returner swiftly garnered national attention. He was awarded the Heisman Trophy in 1939, a testament to his exceptional performance and dedication to the sport and a particular source of pride for the largely agricultural fanbase in Iowa. Kinnick's remarkable on-field achievements solidified his place in the history of college football, earning him a place among the sport's most illustrious figures but his off-field heroics endeared his legacy even greater.

Kinnick was a scholar, excelling academically as well as athletically, epitomizing the ideals of the student-athlete. His commitment to his studies, despite the demands of his athletic career, underscored his dedication to personal excellence in all aspects of his life. Kinnick's unwavering commitment to academic pursuits serves as a testament to the importance of a well-rounded education and the pursuit of knowledge alongside athletic achievements.

Moreover, Kinnick's life was characterized by a profound sense of integrity and humility. His down-to-earth demeanor and selfless attitude endeared him to his teammates, coaches, and fans alike. Kinnick's humility and sportsmanship were legendary, reflecting his deep-rooted values and ethical principles. His integrity on and off the field continues to inspire athletes to uphold the highest standards of sportsmanship and fair play, leaving an indelible mark on the ethos of collegiate sports.

During his acceptance speech of the Heisman Trophy at the historic Downtown Athletic Club in New York City, Kinnick referenced the ability to play football in light of the war in Europe that did not yet involve the United States:

"Finally, if you'll permit me, I'd like to make a comment which in my mind, is indicative perhaps of the greater significance of football, and sports emphasis in general in this country, and that is; I thank God I was warring on the gridirons of the Midwest and not on the battlefields of Europe. I can speak confidently and positively that the players of this country would much more, much rather struggle and fight to win the Heisman award than the Croix de Guerre."

Journalists in attendance were incredibly moved by the young farm boy who turned football hero. Bill Cunningham of the *Boston Post* wrote in response, "This country's okay as long as it produces Nile Kinnick. The football part is incidental." AP reporter Whitney Martin wrote, "You realized the ovation (after his Heisman speech) wasn't alone for Nile Kinnick, the outstanding college football player of the year. It was also for Nile Kinnick, typifying everything admirable in American youth."

Tragically, Kinnick's life was cut short at the age of 24 when his plane crashed during a training flight for the United States Navy in 1943. He had been flying for over an hour when his Grumman F4F Wildcat developed an oil leak so serious that he could neither reach land nor the *Lexington*, whose flight deck was already crowded with planes preparing for launch anyway. He followed standard military procedure and executed an emergency landing in the water but died in the process. Rescue boats arrived on the scene eight minutes later but found only an oil slick. His body was never recovered. He was one month and seven days away from his 25th birthday and was the first Heisman Trophy winner to die.

Despite his premature passing, Kinnick's legacy continues to resonate, serving as a reminder of the

Nile Kinnick with his Heisman Trophy

transformative power of sportsmanship, academic excellence, and personal integrity. His enduring influence remains palpable in the values and principles upheld by athletes, scholars, and individuals committed to making a positive impact on their communities and the world at large. It did not take long for the University of Iowa to rename their football stadium for Nile Kinnick- the only Heisman Trophy winner to have that honor. Before home games the university plays a portion of Kinnick's Heisman Acceptance speech prior to the Star-Spangled Banner.

And so it was that real American heroes like Nile Kinnick guided college football through The Great Depression. Yet College Football was about to face a new type of challenge.

December 7, 1941, rocked the American landscape as Japan deliberately and willfully attacked the United States of America at dawn at the Pearl Harbor Naval Base in Hawaii. America could no longer avoid this World War.

The outbreak of World War II in the 1940s had a profound impact on every facet of American life, and college football was no exception. With the nation's attention turning towards the war effort, the collegiate sports landscape underwent a transformation that would leave an indelible mark on the game for years to come. From the enlistment of players and coaches to the reshaping of the competitive landscape, World War II brought about a significant shift in the dynamics of college football.

One of the most immediate effects of the war was the enlistment of a large number of college football players and coaches into the armed forces. Many young athletes who would have been stars on the gridiron found themselves serving their country on the battlefields of Europe and the Pacific. The departure of these talented individuals from the college football scene significantly depleted the rosters of numerous teams, leading to a decline in the overall quality of play and altering the competitive balance of the sport.

Moreover, the war led to a shortage of resources and personnel that impacted the functioning of colleges and universities across the nation. With many institutions redirecting their focus and resources towards the war effort, the funding and infrastructure required to sustain robust football programs became increasingly scarce. As a result, several colleges were forced to suspend their football programs temporarily, while others struggled to field competitive teams due to a lack of resources and manpower.

The war also brought about significant changes in the structure of collegiate football competitions. Many schools merged their teams with nearby military institutions or formed military training programs on their campuses, leading to the emergence of unique collaborative football initiatives. These collaborations not only helped sustain the sport during the challenging wartime period but also facilitated the development of lasting bonds between colleges and the military that endure to this day.

In addition to these immediate impacts, World War II played a pivotal role in reshaping the cultural significance of college football in American society. College Football, once a primary source of entertainment and communal engagement, took a back seat to the larger concerns of the war effort. The war highlighted the importance of national unity and sacrifice, shifting the public's attention away from recreational activities and towards the collective struggle for freedom and democracy.

Many who made the ultimate sacrifice for their country on the battlefield were well known on the playing field at home.

The three lieutenants moved into a tent on Guadalcanal together. They were platoon leaders in D Company of the 29th Regiment's 2nd Battalion. They also happened to be three well-known college football players at home. "Irish" George Murphy had been Notre Dame's 1942 Team Captain. Walter "Bus" Bergman, a native of Denver, Colorado, had won 10 letters as a star running back at Colorado A&M while also playing basketball and baseball in Fort Collins. Dave Mears had been a standout lineman at Boston University.

The three young men became fast friends. When Murphy received photos of his newborn child, he was quick to share them with Bergman and Mears while chatting about how great it would be when he could finally meet his son. The men knew that advancement to the front and violent battle against the Japanese army awaited them. They did what seemed best to them to be able to forget the war that raged- they organized a football game.

Terry Frei described what became known as the Football Classic of Christmas Eve 1944 in a history penned for ESPN after interviews of living members in 2004:

"Crowd estimates ranged from 2,500 to 10,000. With no bleachers, Marines -- many of whom had placed wagers on the outcome- scrambled to stake out vantage points.

Bergman started in the 29th's backfield, with halfback Bud Seelinger, formerly of Wisconsin; fullback Tony Butkovich, the nation's leading rusher in 1943 at Purdue and the Cleveland Rams' No. 1 draft choice in 1944; and quarterback Frank Callen, from St. Mary's of California. Murphy was one end and player-coach Chuck Behan, formerly of the Detroit Lions, was the other.

It was supposed to be touch football.

The rugged Marines, of course, mostly ignored that

restriction.

John McLaughry, a former Brown University star and ex-New York Giant in the 4th Regiment, served as a playing assistant coach. He wrote to his parents the day after the game, saying: "It was really a Lulu, and as rough hitting and hard playing as I've ever seen. As you may guess, our knees and elbows took an awful beating due to the rough field with coral stones here and there, even though the 29th did its best to clean them all up. My dungarees were torn to hell in no time, and by the game's end my knees and elbows were a bloody mess."

The game ended in a tie. With the considerable amount of money that was bet on the game, the officers in charge were surely grateful for the tie. For one moment on a Christmas Eve in the South Pacific, young men were able to forget the inevitable battle and carnage that awaited them on humid, bug infested jungle islands.

Bergman and his Sixth Division continued training and left for Okinawa. The Marines landed on Easter Sunday, April 1, 1945, and took the beach unopposed. The Japanese had secretly pulled their men from Okinawa in order to fortify other locations. Bergman and his men were relieved. Murphy and Mears would not be so lucky.

Murphy and Mears both arrived at Sugar Loaf Hill on May 15, 1945. Mears was struck by a machine gun bullet in the thigh entering the theater and was immediately removed from battle and transferred to Guam the following day. The clean shot through his thigh likely saved his life.

"Irish" George Murphy, facing incredible odds, ordered a fixed bayonet charge of the Japanese and true to character led the charge. When it became apparent that the losses were too heavy and the objective unlikely, Murphy ordered a retreat and continued to run back and save fallen brothers while carrying them to safety. The official logs of the battle follow what happened next:

"The Marines reached the top and immediately became involved in a grenade battle with the enemy," the combat historians wrote. "Their supply of 350 grenades was soon exhausted. Lieutenant Murphy asked his company commander, Capt. Howard L. Mabie, for permission to withdraw, but Captain Mabie ordered him to hold the hill at all costs. By now the whole forward slope of Sugar Loaf was alive with gray eddies of smoke from mortar blasts, and Murphy ordered a withdrawal on his own initiative. Covering the men as they pulled back down the slope, Murphy was killed by a fragment when he paused to help a wounded Marine."

The story of Notre Dame's Team Captain and Hero was carried in newspapers across the country. With the common line in every major newspaper:

"Irish George staggered to his feet, aimed over the hill and emptied his pistol in the direction of the enemy. Then he fell dead."

Lieutenant Irish George Murphy never met his newborn child. He was one of ten former college football players from the Football Classic of Christmas Eve 1944 on Guadalcanal to lose his life that Spring. The others included:
1. Tony Butkovich, the nation's leading rusher in 1943 from Purdue
2. Bob Baumann, Wisconsin
3. Bob Fowler, Michigan
4. John Hebrank, Lehigh
5. Hubbard Hinde, Southern Methodist

6. Rusty Johnston, Marquette
7. Johnny Perry, Wake Forest
8. Jim Quinn, Amherst
9. Ed Van Order, Cornell

In all, 2,938 Marines were killed in the battles around Okinawa. The Army lost 4,675. In the end, the United States forces were victorious and claimed all of Okinawa, including Sugar Loaf Hill.

Mears returned to his home in Massachusetts after the war and became a CPA. He lived into his late 80's and never forgot The Football Classic.

Bergman returned home to Colorado A&M which is now known as Colorado State. He earned a Master's Degree and started a coaching career at Fort Lewis College in Durango, CO. He later moved to Mesa College in Grand Junction, CO, where he coached both football and baseball. He retired in 1974 but was inducted into the Colorado Sports Hall of Fame in 1995. In 2003, he visited Washington DC and the World War II Memorial for the first time. He found the markers for Okinawa and Guadalcanal. He remembered his friend Irish George and so many others and he wept.

Over 400,000 Americans were killed during World War II. It was estimated that nearly 300 American young men died per day. 3% of the population of the United States died during the war fought by the greatest generation to save global freedom and democracy. As Americans began to return home at the conclusion of the war, they found a game that had managed to survive and was poised to face some of its greatest challenges and opportunities yet as a nation came to grips with what it meant for all men to truly be created equally.

In the aftermath of World War II, the United States witnessed a surge of returning veterans seeking to rebuild their lives and pursue higher education. The implementation of the Servicemen's Readjustment Act of 1944, commonly known as the GI Bill, not only provided educational opportunities for millions of veterans but also catalyzed a transformative shift in the landscape of collegiate football, shaping the sport in profound ways and leaving an enduring legacy of athletic excellence and social mobility.

The GI Bill's provisions, offering financial assistance for education, housing, and vocational training, enabled a significant number of war veterans to enroll in colleges and universities across the nation. This influx of talented and motivated individuals into the collegiate setting breathed new life into college football programs, infusing teams with a wealth of experience, discipline, and leadership skills cultivated during their military service.

The impact of the GI Bill on college football was multifaceted. The integration of seasoned veterans into football programs not only elevated the overall skill level and competitiveness of teams but also instilled a culture of teamwork, resilience, and perseverance that became synonymous with the spirit of the sport. The disciplined approach and strategic acumen honed on the battlefields translated seamlessly onto the football field, fostering a new era of athletic excellence and tactical sophistication within the game.

Moreover, the GI Bill's influence extended beyond the realms of sports, serving as a catalyst for social mobility and economic empowerment. Many veterans who participated in college football programs under the provisions of the GI Bill went on to establish successful careers in various fields, leveraging the skills and values acquired on the gridiron to excel in their chosen professions. The GI Bill's role in fostering opportunities for upward mobility and personal development remains an integral part of the legacy of collegiate football in the post-World War II era.

9 A BARRIER TO BE BROKEN

"Maybe tomorrow we'll all wear 42 so they can't tell us apart."
Pee Wee Reese

Released in 2013, "42" stands as a cinematic testament to the life and legacy of the iconic baseball player, Jackie Robinson. Directed by Brian Helgeland, the film masterfully captures the essence of Robinson's indomitable spirit, his struggle against racial prejudice, and his groundbreaking journey as the first African American to play in Major League Baseball.

The film delves into the pivotal years of Robinson's life, portraying his entry into the Brooklyn Dodgers in 1947 under the guidance of the visionary team executive, Branch Rickey, portrayed brilliantly by Harrison Ford. Chadwick Boseman's mesmerizing performance as Jackie Robinson offers a poignant portrayal of the challenges and triumphs Robinson experienced as he navigated the treacherous waters of racial discrimination in a predominantly white sport.

"42" provides a gripping narrative that showcases the courage and resilience of Jackie Robinson in the face of adversity. The film adeptly captures the deep-seated racial prejudices prevalent in 1940s America, portraying the hostility and bigotry Robinson encountered both on and off the baseball field. The emotional intensity of the film is heightened by its authentic depiction of the struggles Robinson faced, highlighting the emotional toll of being a trailblazer for racial integration in professional sports.

Beyond its portrayal of Robinson's personal journey, "42" serves as a powerful commentary on the transformative power of sports in promoting social change. Robinson's tenacious spirit and unwavering commitment to excellence challenged the status quo and paved the way for greater inclusivity and diversity in the world of baseball. The film's narrative not only celebrates Robinson's exceptional athletic abilities but also underscores the profound impact of his actions on the broader civil rights movement, emphasizing the significance of his role in shaping the course of American history.

"42" transcends its role as a sports biopic, resonating with audiences on a deeper level through its poignant exploration of themes such as perseverance, courage, and the enduring quest for social justice. The film's timeless message of unity and equality remains relevant in contemporary society, serving as a reminder of the importance of breaking down barriers and fostering a more inclusive and equitable world for future generations.

The film leaves out one important fact. Baseball might have been Jackie Robinson's fourth best sport. Before Jackie Robinson made history as the first African American to play in Major League Baseball, he left an indelible mark on the sports landscape at the University of California, Los Angeles (UCLA). Robinson's time at UCLA not only showcased his exceptional athletic abilities but also underscored his pioneering spirit and unwavering commitment to excellence across multiple sports, solidifying his status as a true sporting legend.

During his tenure at UCLA from 1939 to 1941, Robinson's remarkable athleticism and versatility shone brightly as he excelled in an impressive array of sports, including baseball, football, basketball, and track and field. His dynamic presence on the field, court, and track earned him widespread recognition and admiration, laying the foundation for his future success as a trailblazer in professional sports.

Robinson's prowess on the baseball diamond was evident from the outset, as he quickly established himself as a standout player for the UCLA Bruins baseball team. His exceptional batting skills, combined with his agility and speed, made him a formidable force in the college baseball circuit, garnering attention from professional scouts and setting the stage for his groundbreaking career in the major leagues.

In addition to his baseball achievements, Robinson's contributions to UCLA's football, basketball, and track and field teams were equally impressive. As a quarterback and running back for the football team, his exceptional speed and agility enabled him to make significant contributions to the Bruins' offensive prowess. His dynamic abilities on the basketball court and his stellar performances in track and field events further solidified his reputation as a multi-talented athlete with an unparalleled drive for success.

Robinson's trailblazing achievements at UCLA not only demonstrated his exceptional athletic prowess but also exemplified his resilience and determination in the face of racial adversity. Despite the challenges of systemic racism and discrimination, Robinson's unwavering commitment to excellence and sportsmanship served as a beacon of hope and inspiration for future generations of athletes, transcending the confines of sports and making a profound impact on the broader struggle for racial equality.

In Robinson's final football season at UCLA he led the Bruins in rushing (383 yards), passing (444 yards), total offense (827 yards), scoring (36 points) and punt return average (21 yards). He averaged 5.9 yards per carry in his career. Needless to say, coaches and athletic directors across the county began to take notice.

College Football fields in the 1940s and 1950s were like most of America- predominantly segregated. There were others before Robinson but it certainly was not widespread. Fritz Pollard stands as a trailblazer whose contributions to the world of collegiate football transcended the confines of the gridiron. Pollard's groundbreaking achievements in the early 20th century not only shattered racial barriers in college football but also paved the way for a more inclusive and diverse sporting landscape, leaving an enduring legacy of resilience and leadership.

Born on January 27, 1894, in Chicago, Illinois, Pollard's journey to greatness was marked by numerous challenges and obstacles, particularly in the face of systemic racial discrimination. Despite the prevalent racial prejudices of his time, Pollard's exceptional athletic abilities propelled him to the forefront of collegiate sports, where he would eventually leave an indelible mark on the history of football.

Pollard's legacy in college football is best exemplified by his pioneering achievements at Brown University. In 1915, he became the first African American to play in the Rose Bowl, cementing his status as a trailblazer for racial integration in one of the most prestigious collegiate football competitions in the nation. His unparalleled speed, agility, and strategic prowess on the field not only earned him the admiration of fans and teammates but also challenged the deeply entrenched racial stereotypes that pervaded the sporting world. Beyond his groundbreaking achievements on the field, Pollard's influence extended to his later endeavors as a coach and advocate for diversity in sports. His coaching career at historically black colleges and universities (HBCUs) further underscored his commitment to nurturing young talents and fostering a more inclusive environment within collegiate sports. Pollard's advocacy for racial equality and his unwavering dedication to promoting diversity and inclusivity served as a catalyst for the eventual dismantling of racial barriers in the realm of college football.

Pollard's lasting impact on the world of sports continues to resonate in contemporary discussions about the importance of diversity, representation, and equal opportunities in athletics. His pioneering efforts paved the way for future generations of African American athletes, empowering them to pursue their athletic aspirations and contribute to the rich tapestry of collegiate sports in the United States.

Yet perhaps one of the most difficult places for the racial barrier to be broken was in the deep south. The 1950s and 1960s marked a growing era for college football in the Southeastern Conference (SEC), as teams from the region vied for dominance on the gridiron, captivating fans with their unparalleled skill and tenacity. Against the backdrop of a changing America, SEC football emerged as a cultural phenomenon, fostering a sense of pride and camaraderie among communities and redefining the standards of excellence in collegiate sports.

During this remarkable decade, powerhouse teams such as the University of Alabama, the University of Tennessee, and the University of Georgia etched their names in the annals of college football history, showcasing a level of athleticism and sportsmanship that captivated the nation. Coaches like Bear Bryant, Robert Neyland, and Wally Butts emerged as legendary figures, guiding their respective teams to unparalleled success and cementing their places as some of the most influential leaders in the world of collegiate athletics.

The 1950s and 1960s saw a remarkable series of fierce rivalries and nail-biting matchups that exemplified the spirit of competitive excellence within the SEC. From the legendary showdowns between Alabama and Tennessee to the intense clashes between Georgia and Auburn, each game epitomized the grit and determination of the players and coaches, drawing in passionate fans from across the region and beyond.

The unparalleled fervor and devotion of the SEC fan base became a defining characteristic of the conference's football culture in the 1950s and 1960s. Packed stadiums reverberated with the cheers and chants of loyal supporters, creating an electrifying atmosphere that added to the allure and excitement of each game. The deep-rooted traditions and spirited rivalries that defined SEC football during this era continue to shape the conference's identity and contribute to its enduring legacy in the realm of collegiate sports.

Moreover, the 1950s and 1960s witnessed the emergence of several legendary players who would go on to make significant contributions to the sport. Icons such as Johnny Majors, Zeke Bratkowski, and Pat Dye became synonymous with excellence and sportsmanship, leaving an indelible mark on the SEC's storied football history and setting the stage for future generations of talented athletes to follow.

The summer of 1967 was a tumultuous one in the United States. Brimming with fervent activism, political turbulence, and societal shifts, this period witnessed a series of events that both ignited and challenged the momentum of the Civil Rights Movement. From the eruption of riots to the strengthening calls for racial justice, the summer of 1967 remains a poignant reminder of the challenges and triumphs that shaped the course of the Civil Rights Movement.

The summer of 1967 was characterized by a series of devastating riots that spread across several cities in the United States. These riots were often triggered by deep-rooted racial tensions, economic disparities, and the persistent systemic discrimination faced by African Americans. One of the most notorious of these riots was the Detroit riot, which erupted on July 23rd, 1967, after a police raid on an after-hours bar in a predominantly Black neighborhood. The subsequent days witnessed intense clashes between the police and the local community, resulting in widespread violence, destruction, and loss of life.

The impact of the 1967 riots on public perception was profound. While some viewed the riots as expressions of collective frustration and long-standing grievances against systemic racism, others saw them as destabilizing acts that threatened the social fabric. These events underscored the urgency of addressing the systemic issues that perpetuated racial inequality, prompting a deeper examination of the root causes of racial tensions and the inadequacies of existing civil rights policies.

Amidst the turmoil, the summer of 1967 also witnessed heightened activism and mobilization within the Civil Rights Movement. Leaders such as Martin Luther King Jr. and Malcolm X continued to advocate for racial equality and justice, emphasizing the need for systemic reforms. Grassroots organizations and community leaders played a crucial role in organizing protests, advocating for policy changes, and empowering local communities to demand their rights and dignity.

It was in that window of American history that a young man prepared to make his mark on the famed Southeastern Conference during the Fall of 1967. It was at that time that a little-known player with a 3-minute stint in a game between the University of Kentucky and the University of Mississippi changed the conference forever. Nate Northington's appearance on the field for the University of Kentucky marked the first time an African American player appeared in an SEC football game. The barrier was broken.

The University of Kentucky commemorated the moment with a statue of Northington on the 50th Anniversary of the game. It was not a moment that came about easily on that fall day in 1967. Although The Big Ten had opened its lineups to African Americans the SEC had not done so yet.

Northington, a Louisville native, was being heavily recruited by Purdue in The Big Ten. He and his family were invited to Frankfort, Kentucky, for dinner at the Governor's Mansion. It was at that dinner that Kentucky Governor Ned Breathitt asked the Northington family to consider integrating the University of Kentucky and the SEC.

The Northington family was rightfully concerned. The idea of traveling to SEC road games in the deep South presented not just concerns- but actual fears. The Governor promised that Nate would not have to bear the burden alone. Northington's good friend, Greg Page, was also offered a scholarship to attend the University of Kentucky.

The two were inseparable and excited to bring real change following the hot summer of 1967. It would not be. Page was injured in practice in September and tragically passed away on September 29, 1967, the day before the team's second game. With the encouragement of Page's family, Northington took the field with the Wildcats on September 30, 1967, and forever altered the color of the

Southeastern Conference.

5 decades later Northington had the opportunity to be on hand for the unveiling of the statue and to celebrate the anniversary. He walked with his family on gameday on the traditional path from their tailgate to the stadium and passed the statue. He said this in a 2018 interview:

"For the younger people in my family, it gives them a sense of pride of what we accomplished…They've heard the stories, and now they're able to see the statue and to be there at this ceremony. Being there speaks volumes."

Northington did not integrate the SEC by himself. Even further south there was a famed coach who knew he needed to integrate his program to continue to compete for national prominence. Bear Bryant was a fixture of football nationally and in the prominent Southeastern Conference. He knew he needed the right player to be able to endure the treatment he would experience in the deep South. He found that player in John Mitchell.

Amidst the backdrop of the civil rights movement, Mitchell's arrival at the University of Alabama in 1971 marked a transformative moment in the institution's history. His exceptional talent and unwavering determination on the field served as a testament to the power of sports in transcending social boundaries and fostering unity within the community. Mitchell's actions not only inspired his teammates but also galvanized the broader college football landscape, igniting conversations about the importance of diversity and representation in collegiate athletics.

Mitchell's journey at Alabama was not without its challenges. Facing pervasive racial prejudices and systemic barriers, he demonstrated remarkable resilience and fortitude, serving as a beacon of hope and inspiration for individuals striving for equality and justice. His commitment to excellence and sportsmanship transcended the confines

GameDay- The Untold Story of College Football

John Mitchell with Alabama Teammates

of the football field, highlighting the transformative power of athletic prowess in promoting social change and fostering a more inclusive and equitable society.

Furthermore, Mitchell's trailblazing efforts paved the way for future generations of African American athletes to pursue their athletic aspirations and make meaningful contributions to collegiate sports in the Deep South. His legacy at the University of Alabama serves as a testament to the enduring spirit of progress and inclusivity, emphasizing the importance of breaking down barriers and fostering a more welcoming and diverse environment within collegiate athletics.

Because of heroes like Robinson, Pollard, Northington, Mitchell and so many more, the game advanced to new heights in the decade to come. Without the sacrifices of brave young men throughout the fight for equality the country would have never known Bo Jackson, Deion Sanders, Hershall Walker, Eddie George or countless other players who would impact the game of college football for decades to come.

10 THE BEAR

"In life you'll have your back up against the wall many times. You might as well get used to it."
Paul "Bear" Bryant

The 1982 season had not gone the way anyone imagined. A 6th place conference finish was not the standard for the program and the legendary coach was feeling the weight of the world in his health. The private plane touched down on the small airstrip and he waited impatiently for his guest to arrive for their arranged meeting. It wasn't that he feared death itself but as with everything in his life he wanted a game plan.

Robert Schuller, the nationally known evangelist and celebrity in his own right boarded the plane with a smile and a handshake. There is little historical record of the conversation that followed but many close to Bear Bryant would later describe it as a defining point in the late years of Bear's life.

Finishing 6th in the conference was not what killed Bear Bryant, but it certainly didn't help. The legendary coach suffered from the effects of smoking and drinking far too much during his life. Once the image of physical fitness, his legendary jackets now fit a little tighter. At the conclusion of the season, he informed the school and public that the school deserved better than what he could provide as head coach at the University of Alabama.

In his 1983 work, Tears Fall On Alabama, Tom Callahan, recorded a conversation from the retirement press conference. Bryant was asked what he would do now that he was retired. The coach responded, "Probably croak in a week."

Paul William "Bear" Bryant was dead in less than a month. It is truly impossible to discuss College Football in the 20th Century without the words "Bear Bryant."

Born on September 11, 1913, in Moro Bottom, Arkansas, Paul William Bryant grew up in a rural setting shaped by the hardships of the Great Depression. He was the 11th of 12 children and displayed an early affinity for sports, particularly football, during his time at Fordyce High School, where he excelled as a multi-sport athlete. Despite his undeniable talent, Bryant's family faced financial constraints, compelling him to work several odd jobs to support his education and contribute to the family's income.

Bryant accepted a scholarship to play for the University of Alabama in 1931. Since he elected to leave high school before completing his diploma, Bryant had to enroll in a Tuscaloosa high school to finish his education during the fall semester while he practiced with the college team. Bryant played end for the Crimson Tide and was a participant on the school's 1934 national championship team.

Bryant was the self-described "other end" during his playing years with the team, playing opposite the big star, Don Hutson, who later became a star in the National Football League and a Pro Football Hall of Famer. Bryant himself was second team All-Southeastern Conference in

1934, and was third team all-conference in both 1933 and 1935.

He played with a partially broken leg in a 1935 game against Tennessee. Bryant was a member of Sigma Nu fraternity, and as a senior, he married Mary Harmon, which he kept a secret since Alabama did not allow active players to be married.

Bryant was selected in the fourth round in the 1936 NFL Draft, but he never played professional football.

Bryant's coaching career began to take shape during his tenure as an assistant coach at the University of Alabama under head coach Frank Thomas in the late 1930s. His exceptional coaching acumen and leadership skills quickly garnered attention, leading to his eventual promotion to head coach at the University of Maryland in 1945.

In 1946, Paul "Bear" Bryant assumed the role of head coach at the University of Kentucky, marking the beginning of a transformative chapter in the school's football history. Bryant inherited a team that had been struggling to make a mark in the competitive Southeastern Conference (SEC). His arrival infused the program with a renewed sense of purpose and direction, laying the groundwork for a paradigm shift that would redefine Kentucky's approach to the sport.

Bryant's tenure at Kentucky was characterized by a remarkable revitalization of the football program. His emphasis on discipline, rigorous training, and a strategic approach to the game transformed the team's dynamics and elevated its performance to new heights. By instilling a culture of hard work, determination, and a commitment to excellence, Bryant inspired his players to exceed their potential and compete at the highest level, setting a precedent for future success.

Under Bryant's tutelage, the University of Kentucky

football team underwent a significant transformation, both on and off the field. His coaching philosophy centered on fostering a winning mentality that transcended the game itself, emphasizing the values of teamwork, perseverance, and sportsmanship. Bryant's visionary leadership instilled a sense of pride and resilience within the team, galvanizing players to strive for greatness and uphold the highest standards of athletic and personal integrity.

Bryant's tenure at Kentucky left an enduring legacy of excellence that continues to resonate within the university's football program. His unwavering commitment to fostering a culture of discipline and determination laid the foundation for future successes, shaping the ethos of the program for years to come. The principles of hard work, resilience, and a relentless pursuit of greatness that Bryant instilled in his players remain integral to the university's football culture, serving as a testament to his enduring influence.

While Bryant's coaching career at the University of Kentucky spanned a relatively brief period, his transformative influence set the stage for his subsequent achievements at the University of Alabama. The lessons learned and experiences gained during his time at Kentucky undoubtedly played a pivotal role in shaping his coaching philosophy and strategic approach, ultimately contributing to the unparalleled success he would achieve later in his career.

The 1951 Sugar Bowl marked Kentucky's first major bowl game appearance in the program's history, and the team's journey to the championship was fraught with challenges and obstacles. Under Bear Bryant's tutelage, the Wildcats had undergone a rigorous transformation, embracing a culture of discipline, perseverance, and unwavering commitment to excellence. Bryant's coaching philosophy had instilled a sense of resilience within the team, fostering a collective determination to overcome adversity and compete at the highest level.

In the Sugar Bowl matchup against the formidable Oklahoma Sooners, the Kentucky Wildcats demonstrated unwavering tenacity and a steely resolve to emerge victorious. The game itself was a testament to the Wildcats' unyielding spirit, as they overcame a fiercely competitive Oklahoma team to secure a resounding 13-7 triumph. The victory not only solidified Kentucky's place as a force to be reckoned with in collegiate football but also underscored the transformative impact of Bear Bryant's coaching acumen and leadership on the team's success. It was Kentucky's only National Championship.

Legend, folklore, truth and myth surround the circumstances of Bear Bryant's departure from Kentucky. Some claim that the football coach was offered a watch for winning the National Championship while legendary basketball coach Adolph Rupp was offered a car at the same time. Others claim the story is nothing more than a fable. Whatever the truth, Bryant left soon for Texas A&M.

Upon his arrival at Texas A&M, Bear Bryant inherited a football program in need of rejuvenation and direction. In the face of various challenges, including a lack of consistent success and a demanding fan base, Bryant swiftly set about implementing his transformative vision. Central to his coaching philosophy was an emphasis on discipline, hard work, and a commitment to excellence both on and off the field. Bryant's unwavering dedication to instilling these values within his players would become the cornerstone of his legacy at Texas A&M.

Many around the program- including his assistance coaches- thought the coach was too hard on the players. They claimed the practices were too brutal and the hours too long. It did little to deter Bryant's drive of himself and the players.

When Bryant arrived in College Station on February 8, 1954, he felt that most of the boys on the team were undisciplined and exhibited a weakness that would not work in his program. He learned that Texas A&M had a 411-acre campus in the small Texas hill country town of Junction, Texas. Bryant decided to take his team for a football camp in Junction. The members of the team who survived the camp would become known as The Junction Boys.

The brutal 10 day camp became the subject of a 2001 book by Jim Dent, *The Junction Boys*, and a television movie with the same title produced by ESPN, starring Tom Berenger as Bryant. The summer of 1954 featured brutal heat and a severe drought in the hill country of Texas. Coach Bryant led a group of 111 young football players to a remote and unforgiving training camp in Junction, Texas. The rigorous and relentless training regimen, characterized by sweltering heat, grueling practices, and intense physical conditioning, was designed to forge a team of disciplined and resilient athletes capable of withstanding the challenges of competitive collegiate football. Despite facing overwhelming physical and mental hardships, the Junction Boys demonstrated unwavering determination, teamwork, and camaraderie, laying the foundation for a legacy that would transcend the realm of sports.

The punishing training camp, marred by scorching temperatures, dehydration, and exhaustive drills, pushed the players to the brink of their capabilities, demanding unwavering resilience and a relentless commitment to excellence. The relentless perseverance displayed by the Junction Boys amid such adversity epitomized their unwavering dedication to the pursuit of athletic excellence and set a precedent for future generations of Texas A&M football players.

Despite the harsh and demanding conditions of the training camp, the Junction Boys' experience fostered a deep sense of camaraderie, solidarity, and mutual respect among the players. The shared hardships and collective challenges they faced created an unbreakable bond that transcended individual differences and forged a sense of unity and purpose within the team. The camaraderie and team spirit cultivated during the Junction Boys' training camp underscored the significance of collective determination, mutual support, and the enduring power of teamwork in the realm of collegiate athletics.

Practices began before dawn and usually lasted all day, with meetings in the evening until 11pm. The oppressive heat combined with the brutal practice schedule was too much for many of the players. Each day, fewer and fewer players reported for practice, as many quit the team from illness or disgust. The situation was compounded by Bryant's refusal to allow water breaks. This practice, now widely recognized as dangerous, was at the time commonly employed by coaches at all levels in an attempt to "toughen up" their players. The only relief provided to the players were two towels soaked in cold water; one towel was shared by the offensive players, and one by the defense. One of the Junction Boys, future NFL coach Jack Pardee, later said in an interview that some players sweated away 10% of their body weight.

The legacy of the Junction Boys continues to resonate within the halls of Texas A&M University, serving as a timeless reminder of the values of perseverance, discipline, and sacrifice that define the spirit of Aggie football. The lessons learned from their arduous training camp have permeated the culture of Texas A&M athletics, emphasizing the importance of resilience, camaraderie, and a relentless pursuit of excellence both on and off the field. The enduring legacy of the Junction Boys remains a symbol of the enduring spirit and enduring legacy of Texas A&M football, inspiring future generations of athletes to embody the resilience, fortitude, and unwavering commitment to success that define the spirit of the Aggies although it most certainly would not be allowed in today's world of college football coaching and oversight.

The grueling camp and conditions did not translate into immediate success. The Aggies won only one of their ten games that season. It was the only losing season in Bryant's 38 years as a head coach. The Aggies' only victory was a 6–0 win over Georgia on October 2, the third game of the season.

Texas A&M did significantly better the next two seasons, going 7–2–1 in 1955, and 9–0–1 in 1956, winning the Southwest Conference despite being on probation.

Two of the Junction Boys, Jack Pardee and Gene Stallings, went on to become head coaches in the National Football League (NFL). Pardee was a two-time All-Pro with the 1963 Los Angeles Rams and the 1971 Washington Redskins. Stallings also became Texas A&M head coach, and his Aggie team beat Bryant's Alabama team in the 1968 Cotton Bowl Classic. Stallings later became head coach at Alabama and won a national championship in his third season in with the 1992 Crimson Tide, which was Alabama's first national championship following Bryant's death.

Under Bryant's tutelage, the Aggies underwent a remarkable transformation. His rigorous training regimens and meticulous attention to detail elevated the team's performance to new heights, setting a precedent for excellence that would define the program for years to come. By instilling a culture of perseverance, resilience, and a relentless pursuit of greatness, Bryant inspired his players to surpass their potential and compete at the highest level, thereby reinvigorating the spirit of the Aggie football program.

However, it was his return to the University of Alabama as head coach in 1958 that would define his legacy and solidify his status as a coaching legend. It was there he would become the man in the legendary hat and jacket.

From 1958 to 1982, Bryant's tenure as the head coach of the University of Alabama football team witnessed an unprecedented era of success, marked by numerous championships, a transformative coaching philosophy, and an enduring legacy that continues to resonate within the fabric of the university's football heritage.

Upon assuming the role of head coach at the University of Alabama in 1958, Bear Bryant inherited a program seeking a revival and a renewed sense of purpose much like Texas A&M and Kentucky before. His strategic vision and coaching acumen once again swiftly transformed the Crimson Tide into a powerhouse of collegiate football, setting the stage for a period of sustained success and excellence that would come to define the program for generations to come.

When asked why he returned to his alma mater, Bryant replied, "Mama called. And when Mama calls, you just have to come runnin'." Bryant's first spring practice back at Alabama was much like what happened at Junction. Some of Bryant's assistants thought it was even more difficult, as dozens of players quit the team. After winning a combined four games in the three years before Bryant's arrival (including Alabama's only winless season on the field in modern times), the Tide went 5–4–1 in Bryant's first season. The next year, in 1959, Alabama beat Auburn and appeared in the inaugural Liberty Bowl, the first time the Crimson Tide had beaten Auburn or appeared in a bowl game in six years. In the 1960 season, Bryant led Alabama to a 8–1–2 record and a #9 ranking in the final AP Poll. In 1961, with quarterback Pat Trammell and football greats Lee Roy Jordan and Billy Neighbors, Alabama went 11–0 and defeated Arkansas 10–3 in the Sugar Bowl to claim the national championship.

Bryant's coaching philosophy emphasized the values of discipline, perseverance, and unwavering commitment to excellence. His emphasis on instilling a culture of hard work, resilience, and a relentless pursuit of greatness became the cornerstone of the Crimson Tide's football ethos. Under his tutelage, the team embraced a winning mentality that transcended the field, shaping the character of its players and instilling in them the values of sportsmanship and integrity.

Throughout his tenure, Bryant led the Crimson Tide to six national championships, solidifying Alabama's reputation as one of the most dominant forces in collegiate football. His strategic brilliance and unparalleled leadership set a standard of excellence that transcended the confines of the sport, underscoring his profound influence on the university and the broader community. Beyond the realm of athletics, Bryant's impact extended to the fabric of the university's culture, fostering a spirit of excellence, resilience, and unity that permeated every aspect of campus life.

Bryant's enduring legacy at the University of Alabama serves as a timeless testament to his transformative influence and the lasting imprint he left on the Crimson Tide football program. His unwavering commitment to fostering a culture of excellence and integrity set the standard for future generations of players, coaches, and fans, instilling in them the values of determination, sportsmanship, and a relentless pursuit of greatness.

As the University of Alabama continues to celebrate Bear Bryant's enduring legacy, his name remains synonymous with excellence, leadership, and the relentless pursuit of greatness. The lessons learned and the values instilled during Bryant's tenure continue to serve as a guiding light for the Crimson Tide community, inspiring individuals to strive for greatness both on and off the field. In retrospect, Bear Bryant's time at the University of Alabama stands as a testament to the transformative power of visionary leadership, unwavering dedication, and a commitment to upholding the highest standards of athletic and personal integrity.

11 TELEVISION & THE WORLDWIDE LEADER

"When you get ninety million people watching a single game on television, it shows you that people need something to identify with."
Joe Paterno

The crowd in attendance at Triborough Stadium on New York City's Randall's Island sat quiet and stunned. Nearly 9,000 people packed the stands September 30, 1939, to see the preseason National Champion favorite Fordham Rams take on the Waynesburg Yellow Jackets. Waynesburg somehow had managed to score first in the first quarter and took a surprising 7-0 lead on the Rams. But the 9,000 in attendance were not the only ones surprised. Those watching the broadcast on NBC across 1,000 television sets across the region were also enthralled by the potential upset.

It was the first televised college football game.

The game came just a month after the Brooklyn Dodgers and Cincinnati Reds were featured in the first televised professional baseball game broadcast in American history. A college baseball game between Princeton and Columbia had become the first sports event televised a mere five months earlier.

None of that mattered to the crowd in attendance or the crowd watching in a thousand homes across the area. What was of interest at this moment was the surprising start to the game. Everyone was silent. Everyone except Bill Stern. Stern was the sole announcer for NBC affiliate station W2XBS.

Bill Stern, became a pioneering figure in the realm of sports broadcasting and revolutionized the way sports were experienced by audiences across the United States. Known for his dynamic voice, engaging commentary, and passion for sports, Stern played a crucial role in popularizing sports broadcasting during the early 20th century. Stern's influential career and his impact on the world of sports commentary are as crucial to the story of the growth of college football as is Walter Camp.

Born on July 1, 1907, in Rochester, New York, Stern developed a deep love for sports from a young age, harboring a particular fascination for baseball and football. His passion for sports eventually led him to pursue a career in broadcasting, where he honed his skills as a commentator and storyteller, capturing the excitement and drama of sporting events in a unique and compelling manner. Stern's early experiences as a sports enthusiast provided the foundation for his future success as a prominent sports announcer.

Throughout his career, Stern distinguished himself through his innovative approach to sports commentary, incorporating vivid storytelling, dramatic flair, and a deep understanding of the games into his broadcasts. He pioneered the use of descriptive language and narrative techniques, bringing a sense of immediacy and intensity to his live commentary that captivated audiences and immersed them in the thrill of the sporting events. Stern's ability to convey the energy and emotion of sports through his voice set a new standard for sports broadcasting, laying the groundwork for the modern-day approach to live sports coverage.

Stern's captivating broadcasts and charismatic presence on the airwaves quickly garnered him a wide national audience and made him a household name across the United States. His popular radio show, "The Colgate Sports Newsreel," became a staple for sports enthusiasts, providing them with up-to-date coverage of various sporting events and serving as a platform for Stern to showcase his unparalleled talent for engaging storytelling and dynamic commentary. His distinctive style and passion for sports resonated with listeners, cementing his status as one of the most influential sports announcers of his time.

Bill Stern's contributions to sports broadcasting left an enduring legacy that continues to shape the contemporary landscape of sports media. His innovative approach to live commentary set a precedent for future generations of sports announcers, emphasizing the importance of compelling storytelling and engaging narration in enhancing the spectator experience. Stern's influence extended beyond the realm of sports broadcasting, as he played a pivotal role in popularizing sports culture and fostering a sense of communal excitement and enthusiasm for athletic competition among audiences nationwide.

Without Bill Stern there certainly would never have been a Keith Jackson, Pat Summerall, Al Michaels, Joe Buck, Jim Nantz, Dick Enberg, Mike Tirico, Verne Lundquist, Howard Cosell or many more in football. There would never have been Vin Scully, Marty Brennaman or Caywood Ledford. There would never have been an ESPN, Fox Sports or ESPN College GameDay.

But no one was thinking about any of that or the historical president on that brisk fall morning as Fordham fell behind to the much inferior opponent. For that brief moment it appeared one of the greatest upsets of college football history might happen that day, but it was not to be. Fordham went on to score 34 unanswered points for a 34-7 win.

The broadcast was deemed a success and television executives were quick to want more. On October 28, just a month later, the Kansas State Wildcats took on the venerable Nebraska Cornhuskers in a televised homecoming football game. Within the next two decades, Americans would become enthralled watching football, basketball, baseball and boxing on the screens in their living rooms as the television availability grew.

Following the conclusion of World War II, the 1950s witnessed a surge in technological innovation, particularly in the field of electronics and telecommunications. Television sets, previously a luxury item for affluent households, became more accessible and affordable for the average American consumer, thanks to streamlined manufacturing processes and the widespread commercialization of television production. The introduction of black-and-white screens, improved broadcasting signals, and the emergence of major television networks such as CBS, NBC, and ABC laid the foundation for the rapid integration of television into the fabric of American homes.

The growth of television in American homes during the 1950s had a profound cultural impact, revolutionizing the way people consumed information and entertainment. Television programming evolved from news and informational content to include a diverse range of shows, including sitcoms, dramas, variety shows, and live performances. The popularization of iconic programs such as "I Love Lucy," "The Ed Sullivan Show," and "The Twilight Zone" captivated audiences and transformed television into a central source of entertainment and cultural influence. The widespread adoption of television in American homes during the 1950s revolutionized consumer behavior and advertising practices. The rise of commercial advertising on television introduced audiences to a new form of persuasive marketing, prompting a surge in product promotion and brand awareness. Companies recognized the potential of television as a powerful medium to reach a mass audience, leading to the creation of targeted advertisements that shaped consumer preferences and influenced purchasing decisions. The integration of advertising into television programming paved the way for a consumer-driven economy that continues to define the modern commercial landscape.

The growth of television in American homes also fostered a sense of social connectivity and shared cultural experiences within communities. Families gathered around the television set to watch their favorite shows and favorite teams, fostering a collective sense of entertainment and leisure. Television became a catalyst for social interaction and communal bonding, as individuals engaged in discussions about popular programs and shared their experiences with friends and neighbors. The communal viewing experience facilitated a sense of unity and togetherness, contributing to the development of a shared national identity and cultural cohesion.

The 1960s and 1970s witnessed a significant expansion of college football coverage on broadcast networks, with ABC, CBS, and NBC establishing themselves as the primary platforms for showcasing live games. The introduction of color television further enhanced the viewing experience, allowing fans to immerse themselves in the vibrant and electrifying atmosphere of college football stadiums. The emergence of iconic sports commentators and analysts, such as Keith Jackson and Lindsey Nelson, added a new dimension to the broadcast, transforming college football into a national spectacle that transcended regional boundaries and cultural divides.

The advent of cable television in the 1980s revolutionized the landscape of college football broadcasting and took it to an entirely unimagined passion, providing fans with an extensive array of channels and options for accessing live games and in-depth analysis. ESPN played a pivotal role in popularizing college football through its comprehensive coverage and the introduction of flagship programs like "College GameDay," which became a staple for dedicated fans and casual viewers alike. Additionally, the establishment of conference-specific networks, such as the Big Ten Network and the SEC Network, catered to the fervent fan bases of various college football conferences, fostering a sense of regional pride and loyalty among viewers.

The seeds of ESPN were sown in 1978 when Bill Rasmussen, a former communications executive, sought to create a dedicated television network that would exclusively focus on round-the-clock sports coverage. Rasmussen's vision was to provide audiences with a comprehensive platform for accessing live games, highlights, and sports news, thereby transforming the way sports enthusiasts consumed media. With financial backing from his son Scott Rasmussen and friend Ed Egan, Rasmussen laid the groundwork for what would eventually become a groundbreaking and influential sports media empire.

The early days of ESPN were marked by numerous challenges, including financial constraints, limited resources, and the skepticism of industry insiders. Despite these obstacles, the network forged ahead with a series of innovative strategies, including securing the rights to broadcast NCAA college basketball games and leveraging satellite technology to reach a broader audience. The introduction of original programming, such as "SportsCenter," further distinguished ESPN from its competitors, offering viewers a dynamic and engaging sports news format that quickly gained popularity and critical acclaim.

As ESPN's viewership and influence continued to grow, the network diversified its programming to include a wide range of sports content, including coverage of major league sports, college athletics, international competitions, and niche sporting events. Strategic partnerships with professional sports leagues, such as the NFL, NBA, and MLB, bolstered ESPN's credibility and solidified its position as a premier destination for live sports coverage and analysis. The network's expansion into original documentaries, reality shows, and sports-related films further enhanced its appeal and contributed to its reputation as a comprehensive and multifaceted sports media powerhouse.

ESPN's comprehensive coverage of college football has significantly contributed to the sport's exponential growth in broadcasting and viewership. Through the broadcast of live games, in-depth analysis, and exclusive access to behind-the-scenes content, ESPN has provided fans with an immersive and engaging viewing experience that transcends traditional boundaries. The network's commitment to showcasing a diverse range of college football matchups, including bowl games, rivalry showdowns, and championship tournaments, has solidified its position as the go-to destination for comprehensive and high-quality sports entertainment.

ESPN's extensive coverage of college football has led to

enhanced exposure and brand visibility for collegiate athletic programs, elevating the profiles of universities and their football teams on a national scale. Through its expansive network of channels, including ESPN, ESPN2, and ESPN3, the network has provided smaller and mid-tier college football programs with a platform to showcase their talent and compete with larger, more established institutions. This increased exposure has not only heightened the competitiveness of college football but has also opened new avenues for recruiting and cultivating a broader fan base for various collegiate teams. Perhaps no creation of ESPN has influenced the growth of college football as much as ESPN College GameDay.

ESPN College GameDay originated from a simple vision to create a dynamic and engaging pre-game show that would capture the excitement and fervor surrounding college football. In 1987, the inaugural episode of College GameDay aired, setting the stage for a groundbreaking program that would revolutionize the way fans experienced the anticipation and anticipation leading up to college football matchups. The show's innovative format, featuring insightful analysis, spirited discussions, and interactive fan segments, quickly captured the hearts and imaginations of viewers, laying the foundation for what would become a beloved and enduring sports media franchise.

Over the years, ESPN College GameDay evolved to encompass a diverse range of elements that distinguished it as a premier pre-game show. The introduction of the "Picks Segment," where analysts offered their predictions for the day's key matchups, became a fan-favorite feature that added an element of friendly competition and anticipation to the show. Additionally, the incorporation of on-site fan activities, including sign-making contests, tailgate celebrations, and live interviews with passionate supporters, fostered a sense of inclusivity and community engagement that set College GameDay apart as more than just a pre-game analysis program, but as a cultural event that celebrated the collective spirit of college football fandom. As College GameDay's popularity soared, the show expanded its reach beyond traditional college campuses, visiting various locations across the nation to showcase the rich diversity and fervent enthusiasm of college football fan bases. The program's nationwide tours not only highlighted the cultural significance of college football but also provided a platform for different universities and communities to showcase their unique traditions, spirit, and pride. College GameDay's ability to bring together fans from different regions, backgrounds, and allegiances underscored its role as a unifying force within the broader tapestry of college football culture, promoting a sense of shared excitement and camaraderie that transcended individual team rivalries and regional affiliations.

College GameDay's impact on sports media and fan engagement has been far-reaching, reshaping the way audiences interact with pre-game coverage and analysis. The program's innovative blend of expert commentary, lighthearted banter, and interactive fan participation has set a standard for sports broadcasting that emphasizes the importance of creating a dynamic and inclusive viewing experience for audiences of all ages and backgrounds. College GameDay's influence on fan engagement and the cultivation of a vibrant college football community has underscored the significance of sports media in fostering a sense of shared identity, excitement, and camaraderie among fans and enthusiasts across the nation.

ESPN's influence on college football extends beyond the realm of broadcasting, as the network has fostered a vibrant and inclusive sports culture that resonates with fans of all ages and backgrounds. The network's interactive programming, such as "College GameDay" and "ESPN College Football Primetime," has become a staple for dedicated fans, offering a unique blend of expert analysis, fan engagement, and lively discussions that capture the essence and excitement of college football. These shows have served as a rallying point for fan communities, fostering a shared sense of enthusiasm and camaraderie that transcends geographical boundaries and unites individuals in their passion for the game.

ESPN's involvement in college football has had a significant impact on the monetization and financial growth of collegiate athletic programs. The network's multi-billion-dollar broadcast deals, sponsorship agreements, and advertising partnerships have contributed to the financial sustainability of many colleges and universities, providing vital resources for the development of athletic facilities, recruitment of top-tier coaches and athletes, and the overall advancement of academic and athletic programs. The lucrative nature of ESPN's collaborations with college football has not only elevated the economic viability of collegiate sports but has also underscored the essential role of media partnerships in supporting the long-term success and sustainability of collegiate athletic institutions.

ESPN's enduring impact on college football has reshaped the sport into a cultural phenomenon that transcends athletic competition, becoming a unifying force that brings together communities, fans, and athletes in celebration of teamwork, perseverance, and the spirit of collegiate sportsmanship. Through its comprehensive coverage, innovative programming, and financial support, ESPN has solidified its position as a transformative and influential entity in the realm of college football, leaving an indelible legacy that continues to resonate with audiences and enthusiasts across the nation.

The 2010s marked a transformative period for college football on television, as the proliferation of digital platforms and streaming services reshaped the way fans consumed live games and related content. With the rise of streaming giants like Amazon Prime Video and Netflix, traditional broadcasters and conference networks faced increasing competition in the race to capture the attention of tech-savvy audiences. Consequently, the integration of interactive features, multi-platform accessibility, and personalized viewing experiences became integral to the future of college football broadcasting, as networks sought to engage and retain a diverse and digitally connected fan base.

The evolution of college football on television has had a profound impact on sports culture and the media landscape, solidifying the game's status as a national pastime and a cultural phenomenon. The increased accessibility and widespread coverage of college football have fostered a sense of community and shared identity among fans, transcending geographical barriers and fostering a collective passion for the sport. Moreover, the commercialization of college football on television has transformed it into a lucrative enterprise, with sponsorships, advertisements, and broadcasting rights contributing to the financial growth and sustainability of collegiate athletic programs and institutions.

After the brisk fall morning in Triborough Stadium, Bill Stern continued broadcasting sporting events for nearly two decades. He inspired countless broadcasters outside the world of sports. Paul Harvey drew his inspiration from Stern's style and frequent social commentaries during events. Stern occasionally appeared in feature films as himself. Two of his more familiar credits are *The Pride of the Yankees*, starring Gary Cooper, and *Here Come the Co-Eds*, starring Abbott and Costello. He also narrated a long-running series of 10-minute short subjects for Columbia Pictures, "Bill Stern's World of Sports." He served as sports commentator for News of the Day newsreels, as he acknowledged in his signoff message on his *Colgate Shave Cream Sports Newsreel of the Air* over NBC Radio ("Until then, I'll be seeing you in the News of the Day newsreel at your favorite Loews or Associated theaters!").

In 1984, Bill Stern was part of the American Sportscasters Association Hall of Fame's initial class which also included sportscasting legends Red Barber, Don Dunphy, and Graham McNamee. Stern was inducted into the National Radio Hall of Fame posthumously in 1988 and even has a star in the Hollywood Walk of Fame. Whether Stern understood the impact of the first collegiate football game broadcast or not that day, it is undeniable the impact it had on the growth of the sport and the creation of so many voices who have become iconic members of living rooms around the country throughout the last century.

12 HEISMAN

"Every kid thinks about the Heisman Trophy and dreams about it, but you never think it could happen to you."
Carson Palmer, QB USC, 2002 Heisman Trophy

"What is this? It is a prolate spheroid, an elongated sphere in which the outer leather casing is drawn tightly over a somewhat smaller rubber tubing. Better to have died as a small boy than to fumble this football."

So began the opening monologue of the college football season each year by Coach John Heisman.

The young men leaned in for the brilliance and encouragement of their famed coach.

Born on October 23, 1869, in Cleveland, Ohio, just four years after the completion of The Civil War, Heisman's profound impact on the development and popularization of modern football is still felt today across the landscape and tapestry of college football each fall. From an early age, John Heisman displayed an innate passion and talent for athletics, particularly football. His formative years were characterized by a deep fascination with the sport, as he excelled as a standout player at Brown University, where he played as a lineman, fullback, and center. Heisman's early experiences as a collegiate athlete served as the foundation for his future endeavors as a coach, strategist, and visionary leader within the realm of American football.

Heisman's early coaching career was marked by a series of groundbreaking innovations and strategic advancements that revolutionized the way football was played and coached. His tenure as the head coach at various institutions, including Oberlin College, Buchtel College (now the University of Akron), and the University of Pennsylvania, solidified his reputation as a master tactician and visionary mentor. Heisman's emphasis on strategic gameplay, tactical precision, and innovative offensive formations and the forward pass redefined the sport, laying the groundwork for the modern principles of football strategy and coaching.

The son of Bavarian German immigrants Johann Michael Heissmann and Sara Lehr Heissmann, Johann Wilhelm Heisman, grew up in northwestern Pennsylvania near Titusville. He was salutatorian of his graduating class at Titusville High School. His oration at his graduation ceremony was titled, "The Dramatist as Sermonizer" and he was later described by teachers as "full of dramatic emphasis and fire, and showed how the masterpieces of Shakespeare depicted the ends of unchecked passion."

Although he was a drama student, he often described himself as "football mad." He played varsity football for Titusville High School from 1884 to 1886. Heisman's father refused to watch him play at Titusville, calling football "bestial". Heisman went on to play football as a lineman at Brown University and at the University of Pennsylvania where he also played baseball.

In his book *Principles of Football*, Heisman described his coaching strategy: "The coach should be masterful and commanding, even dictatorial. He has no time to say 'please'

GameDay- The Untold Story of College Football

John Heisman, Brown University

or 'mister'. At times he must be severe, arbitrary, and little short of a czar." Heisman always used a megaphone at practice. "Heisman's voice was deep, his diction perfect, his tone biting." He was also known for his use of polysyllabic language such as the opening lines of the speech that he gave to start each school year.

After two years of coaching at Oberlin the economic Panic of 1893 set in and changed the course of his life. The Panic of 1893, one of the most severe economic crises in American history, remains a pivotal moment that shaped the trajectory of the nation's financial landscape and political discourse. Triggered by a series of complex factors, including overexpansion, railroad failures, and a sharp decline in the gold reserve, the Panic of 1893 led to widespread unemployment, bank failures, and a prolonged period of economic depression.

The origins of the Panic of 1893 can be traced back to a confluence of economic imbalances and vulnerabilities within the American financial system. The collapse of major railroad companies, the diminishing gold reserves, and the overextension of credit contributed to a climate of uncertainty and financial instability, prompting a rapid decline in investor confidence and a subsequent contraction of the economy. The subsequent chain reaction of bank failures, plummeting commodity prices, and a widespread credit crunch sent shockwaves through various sectors of the economy, exacerbating the severity of the crisis and underscoring the interconnectedness of the nation's financial institutions.

The economic upheaval brought about by the Panic of 1893 had a profound impact on industrial workers and farmers, exacerbating existing grievances and disparities within the labor force. Mass unemployment and wage cuts within industrial sectors led to widespread labor unrest and social unrest, as disenfranchised workers and labor unions mobilized to demand fair wages, improved working conditions, and governmental intervention to alleviate the economic hardships faced by working-class families. Similarly, farmers, already grappling with agricultural overproduction and falling crop prices, were further burdened by the economic downturn, leading to widespread foreclosures, farm closures, and rural poverty.

Heisman invested what little savings he had amassed in his young coaching career and began working at a tomato farm in Marshall, Texas. It was hard work in the heat and Heisman soon found he was losing money in the endeavor that his father thought would be safer than coaching. He was contacted by Walter Riggs, then the manager of the Alabama Polytechnic Institute (Auburn University) football team. Auburn was looking for a football coach, and Heisman was suggested to Riggs by one of his former players at Oberlin, Penn's then-captain Carl S. Williams. Heisman accepted the position for a salary of $500, the equivalent of $17,099 in 2023.

Heisman coached football at Auburn for the next four years. Auburn's yearbook, the *Glomerata*, in 1897 stated "Heisman came to us in the fall of '95, and the day on which he arrived at Auburn can well be marked as the luckiest in the history of athletics at the Alabama Polytechnic Institute."

In 1900, Heisman became both the football and baseball coach at Clemson University for a salary of nearly four times what he was paid at Auburn. It was Walter Riggs who once again facilitated the deal as he himself had previously moved from Auburn to Clemson. Heisman still has the highest winning percentages in both football and baseball in Clemson school history. His time at Clemson had significant meaning for him personally as well.

Heisman met his first wife, an actress, while he was participating in theater during his time at Clemson. Evelyn McCollum Cox, whose stage name was Evelyn Barksdale, was a widow with a single child, a 12-year-old boy named Carlisle. They married during the 1903 season, on October 24, 1903, a day after Heisman's 34th birthday. While in Atlanta, Heisman also shared the house with the family poodle named Woo. He would feed the dog ice cream.

In 1918, Heisman and his wife divorced, and to prevent any social embarrassment to his former wife, who chose to remain in the city, he left Atlanta after the 1919 football season. Carlisle and Heisman remained close the rest of their lives.

Four years later Heisman was on the move again. After his Clemson team defeated Georgia Tech 73-0, the Atlanta school offered Heisman a deal that would raise his salary by $50 per month and allow him to receive 30% of the home ticket sales. It was the first of its kind deal. Heisman packed for Atlanta. He coached Georgia Tech for the next 16 years. It was the longest tenure of his coaching career.

Beyond his coaching prowess, John Heisman joined contemporaries such as Walter Camp to make significant contributions to the development of standardized rules and regulations within the realm of American football. His advocacy for player safety, fair play, and ethical sportsmanship led to the implementation of critical rule changes that prioritized the well-being of athletes and promoted a sense of integrity and sportsmanship on the field. Heisman's unwavering commitment to upholding the values of honor, respect, and fair competition has left an indelible mark on the ethos of American football, shaping the culture and principles that continue to define the sport to this day.

Heisman's legacy extends beyond his contributions to the sport of football, encompassing his enduring impact on the lives and careers of countless student-athletes whom he mentored and guided throughout his coaching career. His commitment to fostering a culture of academic excellence, personal growth, and character development among his players exemplified his dedication to nurturing well-rounded individuals who embodied the values of sportsmanship, discipline, and perseverance. Heisman's educational legacy continues to resonate within the collegiate athletics community, inspiring student-athletes to strive for excellence both on and off the field and to uphold the principles of integrity, leadership, and academic achievement.

John Heisman's enduring legacy is perhaps best embodied by the prestigious award that bears his name—the Heisman Trophy. Established in 1935, the Heisman Trophy has become the most coveted individual accolade in college football, honoring the most outstanding player of the season and recognizing excellence, leadership, and athletic prowess. Heisman's legacy as a pioneering figure in American football continues to be celebrated through the annual presentation of the Heisman Trophy, underscoring his enduring influence on the sport and his lasting impact on the lives and careers of countless student-athletes.

The Heisman Trophy, an iconic symbol of individual excellence and athletic achievement in American collegiate football, stands as one of the most prestigious and coveted awards in the realm of sports. First presented in 1935, the Heisman Trophy has come to represent the pinnacle of athletic prowess, leadership, and sportsmanship, honoring the most outstanding college football player of the season.

Established in 1935 by the Downtown Athletic Club of New York City as the Downtown Athletic Club Trophy, the award was initially conceived as a means of recognizing the most outstanding college football player in the nation, commemorating their exceptional performance, leadership, and contribution to the sport. The chairman of the Downtown Athletic Club of New York City? None other than John Heisman. The inaugural award was presented to University of Chicago's Jay Berwanger, setting a precedent for the celebration of athletic excellence that continues to define the Heisman Trophy to this day.

The trophy itself, designed by sculptor Frank Eliscu, is modeled after Ed Smith, a leading player in 1934 for the now-defunct New York University football team. The trophy is made out of cast bronze, is 13.5 inches (34.3 cm) tall, 14 inches long, 16 inches in width and weighs 45 pounds (20.4 kg).

Eliscu had asked Smith, his former George Washington High School classmate, to pose for a commissioned sculpture of a football player. Smith did not realize until 1982 that the sculpture had become the Heisman Trophy. The Downtown Athletic Club presented Smith with a Heisman Trophy of his own in 1985.

From its inception in 1935, the statue was cast by Dieges & Clust in New York (and later Providence, Rhode Island) until 1980, when Dieges and Clust was sold to Herff Jones. For a time until at least 2008, the statues were cast by Roman Bronze Works in New York. Since 2005 the trophy has been made by MTM Recognition in Del City, Oklahoma

The Heisman Trophy embodies the timeless values of dedication, sportsmanship, and athletic prowess, serving as a symbol of individual achievement and collective spirit within the realm of collegiate athletics. The criteria for selecting the Heisman Trophy winner emphasize not only exceptional on-field performance but also leadership, integrity, and a commitment to excellence both as an athlete and as a representative of their respective university. The recipient of the Heisman Trophy is chosen based on their overall impact on the game, their statistical achievements, and their contribution to the success and prestige of their team throughout the football season.

Over the decades, the presentation ceremony of the Heisman Trophy has evolved into a highly anticipated and celebrated event within the realm of collegiate sports. The annual Heisman Trophy presentation, broadcast nationally, has become a hallmark of the college football season, showcasing the achievements and contributions of exceptional student-athletes to a global audience. The ceremony, which includes the unveiling of the Heisman Trophy recipient and their acceptance speech, serves as a platform for athletes to express their gratitude, share their personal journeys, and inspire future generations of aspiring football players to strive for excellence both on and off the field.

The Heisman Trophy's enduring legacy extends beyond the realm of collegiate sports, encapsulating the spirit of determination, perseverance, and sportsmanship that defines the essence of American athletics. The award has become synonymous with the celebration of individual excellence and the promotion of teamwork, discipline, and leadership, fostering a culture of athletic achievement and personal growth among student-athletes nationwide. The Heisman Trophy's cultural impact serves as a testament to the enduring spirit of collegiate athletics, inspiring generations of athletes to embody the values of integrity, dedication, and excellence that define the essence of the Heisman legacy.

Heisman died of pneumonia on October 3, 1936, in New York City. On December 10, 1936, just 2 months after

Heisman's death, the Downtown Athletic Club Trophy was renamed the Heisman Memorial Trophy. He was preparing to write a history of college football at the time of his death and was remembered as a gifted actor, football coach and innovator. He surely had no idea that the trophy in his name would become the most coveted possession for individuals in all of college football.

Heisman was inducted into the College Football Hall of Fame as a coach in 1954, a member of the second class of inductees. Heisman was an innovator and "master strategist". He developed one of the first shifts while being a proponent of the legalization of the forward pass. Heisman had both his guards pull to lead an end run and had his center snap the ball and he invented the hidden ball play while also originating the "hike" shouted by the quarterback to start each play. He led the effort to cut the game from halves to quarters and is credited with the idea of listing downs and yardage on the scoreboard, and of putting his quarterback at safety on defense.

There are remembrances of John Heisman nearly everywhere he coached. Clemson's campus features Heisman Street. Heisman Drive is located on Auburn's campus and a bust of Heisman appears in the Auburn stadium. A bronze statue of Heisman was erected on Akron's campus, and another is located at Georgia Tech University.

The Heisman Trophy is the oldest and most prestigious of the trophies awarded to college football players as individuals. The awards, including the Maxwell Award, Walter Camp Award, and the AP Player of the Year are awarded annual and voted by panelists with various intents. The Heisman and the AP Player of the Year honor the *outstanding player*, while the Maxwell and the Walter Camp award recognizes the *best player*, and the Archie Griffin

Award recognizes the *most valuable player*.

There was no way to know that a small-town thespian from rural northwest Pennsylvania would have such a grand impact on the game of college football and college athletics. Heisman always remembered his roots and kept a sense of humor.

When asked for coaching advice to young coaches shortly before his death, Heisman simply replied, "Don't cuss. Don't argue with the officials. And don't lose the game."

The legacy of an all-time great.

13 SEPTEMBER 11

"I can hear you. The rest of the world hears you. And the people who knocked these buildings down will hear all of us soon."
President George W. Bush, September 14, 2001

"The White House wants y'all to play football."

The surreal words came across the phone from SEC commissioner Roy Kramer to Mississippi State Athletic Director Larry Templeton on Monday, September 17, 2001.

Like everyone else, Templeton was unsure of how to restart life after the deadly terror attacks of September 11, 2001.

The day started normal enough- if not pristine. The Federal Aviation Administration described the day on the east coast as "severe clear." It was a terminology meaning that it was perfect for flight. There was hardly a cloud in any direction as far as the eye could see.

The country went about business as normal. President George W. Bush entered Emma E. Booker Elementary

School to read with young children near Sarasota, FL, as a plane crashed into the World Trade Center.

The President was sitting in Room 301, a second-grade classroom at the school, reading with students when his chief of staff told him about the second crash.

"A second plane has hit the second tower," Andrew Card whispered to him. "America is under attack."

At that moment America changed.

On that severe clear and seemingly ordinary morning of September 11, 2001, the world was abruptly shaken by a series of meticulously planned and coordinated terrorist attacks targeting the heart of American economic and military power. At 8:46 a.m. EDT, American Airlines Flight 11, hijacked by five terrorists, crashed into the North Tower of the World Trade Center in Lower Manhattan, instantly engulfing the building in flames and sending shockwaves of disbelief and horror throughout the nation. Within minutes, the surreal nature of the tragedy intensified as United Airlines Flight 175 struck the South Tower at 9:03 a.m., exacerbating the sense of panic, confusion, and vulnerability that gripped the nation.

While the nation grappled with the chaos and devastation unfolding in New York City, the Pentagon, the nerve center of the United States military, became the next target of the terrorist plot. American Airlines Flight 77, commandeered by five hijackers, crashed into the western side of the Pentagon at 9:37 a.m., causing a catastrophic inferno and claiming the lives of 125 people inside the building, as well as the 59 passengers and crew members on the plane. Simultaneously, United Airlines Flight 93, believed to have been bound for a high-profile target in Washington, D.C., was heroically brought down by passengers who thwarted the hijackers' plans, sacrificing their lives to prevent further destruction and loss of innocent lives.

In the aftermath of the 9/11 attacks, the United States and the international community rallied together in a display of solidarity, compassion, and unwavering support for the victims, their families, and the resilience of the American people. Memorials, candlelight vigils, and moments of silence were observed worldwide, paying tribute to the thousands of lives lost and expressing a collective determination to stand united against the forces of hatred and terror. The outpouring of global support and expressions of solidarity underscored the universal condemnation of terrorism and the collective commitment to upholding the values of peace, tolerance, and respect for human dignity in the face of unspeakable tragedy.

For the first time since the 1940s, college football delayed its season. Every game across the country planned for the following weekend was either cancelled or delayed with no idea of when football would return. There was little pushback. It was, after all, just a game considering the horrific suffering and pain that had been unleashed on the country.

Americans came together like never before to mourn and hold each other up but after a week it was clear to The White House that if life was cancelled for the long-term in America the terrorists had certainly won a victory. It was in that vein that The Bush Administration reached out to Roy Kramer.

The SEC was the largest and most influential conference in college football, and it was clear that others would follow their lead if they began playing again. The Bush Administration also knew that Kramer had been outspoken for the American ways of life to return and continue.

The SEC had a key matchup of two ranked teams on the slate- South Carolina at Mississippi State.

The university athletic directors, Presidents and coaches all expected to be postponed another week when the call came from Kramer on that Monday evening relaying President Bush's desire for Americans to get back to normal life as quickly as possible, including athletics.

Historian Michael Smith recorded what came next in an article for Sports Business Journal commemorating the 20th Anniversary of the game in 2021:

"Templeton had little time to think about the significance of the moment. They were scheduled to play in three days under unprecedented circumstances. Protocols for security had to be rewritten quickly.

We looked at every scenario when it came to moving games around," Womack said. "You take every consideration and put it on the table. We were talking to other conferences, the NFL. We ended up moving (extending) the season back a week.

And then with South Carolina, you had to think about travel and if they'd be OK flying. There were a lot of big decisions that had to be made."

Both schools fully committed to playing that Thursday night.

With just two full days left to prepare for the game, Templeton assembled his staff. The safety of the players, coaches and fans would take the highest priority. Many of the safety precautions that fans take for granted now were instituted for that game."

Fans in Starkville, Mississippi, began to fill the stands that day unsure of what to expect. The volume of the crowd went silent as the video board began a special pre-game segment featuring the play-by-play announcer and ESPN broadcast crew. This was a special moment to memorialize those lost and those who sacrificed. It was clear that the game would be in second place to the feeling of America taking a step forward toward healing that day.

The weeks that followed featured giant flags, patriotic songs and a feeling of warmth even among the most bitter rivals.

The 9/11 attacks marked a turning point in global politics and security, ushering in an era of heightened vigilance, increased intelligence sharing, and a comprehensive reevaluation of international security protocols. The United States, under the leadership of President George W. Bush, declared a "War on Terror," initiating military campaigns in Afghanistan and later in Iraq to dismantle terrorist networks, disrupt their operational capabilities, and prevent the proliferation of extremist ideologies. The global response to 9/11 underscored the imperative of international cooperation and the necessity of collective action to combat the threat of transnational terrorism and uphold the principles of global peace and stability in an increasingly interconnected world.

The experience of 9/11 impacted not only those in the stands but those on the field as well.

Pat Tillman's early years were marked by a deep passion for athletics and a fierce determination to excel on the football field. After an outstanding collegiate career at Arizona State University, where he earned numerous accolades for his exceptional skills as a defensive player, Tillman was drafted by the Arizona Cardinals to fulfill his dream as an NFL football player. His tenure with the Cardinals would be brief but was characterized by a stellar performance, unwavering work ethic, and a profound commitment to teamwork and sportsmanship, earning him the respect and admiration of teammates, coaches, and fans alike. Tillman's dedication to excellence on the football field laid the foundation for his later pursuit of a higher calling—one that would define the essence of his legacy and enduring impact on the world.

In the wake of the tragic events of September 11, 2001, Pat Tillman made the decision to forgo his professional football career and enlist in the United States Army, driven by a deep sense of duty, patriotism, and a desire to contribute to the defense of his country. Tillman's decision to join the Army Rangers exemplified his unwavering commitment to service and his profound belief in the principles of honor, integrity, and selfless sacrifice. His selflessness and courage in the face of adversity and uncertainty served as an inspirational testament to the transformative power of individual conviction and the enduring spirit of patriotism that defines the essence of American citizenship and global solidarity.

Tragically, Pat Tillman's life was cut short while serving in Afghanistan on April 22, 2004. His untimely death shook the nation, the global community and the world of college football, underscoring the profound impact of his sacrifice and the enduring legacy of his commitment to service, integrity, and the pursuit of a higher purpose. Tillman's unwavering dedication to upholding the values of honor, courage, and selflessness continues to resonate within the realms of sports, military service, and civic engagement, serving as a poignant reminder of the transformative power of individual action and the enduring legacy of those who strive to make a meaningful and lasting impact on the world.

Pat Tillman's enduring legacy extends far beyond the realms of sports and military service, encompassing his profound impact on society, global consciousness, and the collective spirit of civic engagement and social responsibility. The Pat Tillman Foundation, established in his honor, has become a beacon of hope and empowerment for aspiring student-scholars, military veterans, and individuals dedicated to making a positive difference in their communities and the world. The foundation's commitment to fostering leadership, academic excellence, and community service reflects Tillman's enduring legacy of service and the transformative power of education in nurturing the next generation of leaders, changemakers, and advocates for social justice and global solidarity.

As the nation grappled with the emotional aftermath of 9/11, college football emerged as a source of solace, inspiration, and healing that transcended the boundaries of sport and united Americans in their pursuit of healing, reconciliation, and renewal. The resumption of college football games in the weeks following the attacks symbolized the nation's resilience and determination to persevere in the face of tragedy, underscoring the integral role of sports in providing a sense of normalcy, hope, and communal strength during tumultuous times. College football's unwavering commitment to promoting a spirit of unity, empathy, and national pride became a source of inspiration for a nation in mourning, serving as a reminder of the enduring power of sports to uplift spirits, heal wounds, and bring communities together in times of adversity.

The legacy of 9/11's impact on college football serves as a poignant reminder of the enduring power of sports in fostering unity, resilience, and social consciousness in the face of national tragedy. The lessons learned from the unifying spirit of collegiate athletics during this tumultuous period underscore the importance of sports as a catalyst for fostering empathy, promoting unity, and advocating for social change in times of crisis. The enduring legacy of 9/11's impact on college football continues to resonate within the collegiate sports community, inspiring future generations of student-athletes, coaches, and fans to embody the values of unity, compassion, and resilience that define the essence of the collegiate sports experience and the enduring spirit of the American nation.

The impact of 9/11 on the fabric of American life is still imprinted over two decades later. The death toll of 9/11 stands as a solemn testament to the devastating impact of terrorism on the lives of innocent civilians, first responders, and individuals from all walks of life. The coordinated attacks on the World Trade Center in New York City, the Pentagon in Washington, D.C., and the crash of United Flight 93 claimed the lives of 2,977 victims, leaving a profound void in the hearts and minds of their loved ones and a nation grappling with incomprehensible grief and sorrow.

The health impacts of the 9/11 attacks on first responders have been far-reaching and enduring, with many individuals experiencing a range of debilitating illnesses, respiratory disorders, and chronic health conditions because of their exposure to toxic dust, fumes, and environmental contaminants at Ground Zero. Respiratory ailments, such as asthma, chronic obstructive pulmonary disease (COPD), and various forms of cancer, have become prevalent among first responders, underscoring the lasting consequences of their selfless sacrifice and unwavering commitment to saving lives in the wake of unprecedented tragedy.

Beyond the numerical representation of the death toll, the human stories and personal narratives of the 9/11 victims serve as a powerful reminder of the diverse tapestry of lives, dreams, and aspirations that were tragically cut short on that fateful day. The stories of heroism, selflessness, and compassion displayed by first responders, civilians, and individuals who sacrificed their lives to save others underscore the profound impact of individual actions and the enduring legacy of courage, empathy, and solidarity that define the essence of the human spirit in times of adversity.

Yet College Football played a small part of healing a broken country that Fall of 2001. Stadiums began to fill in the face of terror. Fans and teams began to fly again. Many young men who would have undoubtedly left their mark on the game of football decided to join a different team and pursue those responsible throughout the mountains and hill country along the borders of Afghanistan and Pakistan.

Two historic phone calls set the healing in motion- The White House to Roy Kramer and Roy Kramer to Mississippi State University. Once again- just as it had in the wake of The Great Depression, World War II, and other 20th Century Conflicts and Cultural Markers- College Football brought unity, healing and a sense of normal to everyday life.

14 A NEW ERA

"My issue with the playoff is that if you lose late in the season it has a much greater impact than if you lose early in the season."
Nick Saban, Alabama Head Coach, 2018

In the years that followed 9/11 one key issue seemed to frequently find itself at the forefront of college football arguments- how do you crown a national champion?

College Football was unique. Other sports had post-season tournaments that featured an elimination process to the eventual champion. College Football was filled with conferences of various strengths and independent bowl games that were often filled from conference affiliation rather than the desire to crown a champion.

The Bowl Championship Series (BCS) stood as the initial attempt to level the college football landscape, tasked with determining the national champion through a complex algorithm and selection process. Despite its initial intent to streamline the championship selection process, the BCS era bore witness to a litany of criticisms, controversies, and inherent flaws that tarnished its reputation and alienated fans, players, and coaches alike. Delving into the reasons why the BCS was detrimental to college football unveils a convoluted narrative of inequity, subjectivity, and a profound disconnect from the sport's fundamental values.

One of the primary grievances levied against the BCS system was its reliance on subjective rankings and polls, which often yielded contentious and disputed outcomes. The amalgamation of human polls, computer rankings, and strength of schedule metrics failed to provide a comprehensive and transparent framework for selecting the top teams, leading to discrepancies and grievances within the college football community. The lack of standardized, objective criteria for evaluating teams' performances sowed seeds of distrust and disillusionment among fans and teams, exacerbating the perceived bias and favoritism inherent in the BCS selection process.

The BCS system's inherent bias and rigidity often led to the exclusion of deserving teams from smaller conferences, perpetuating a sense of inequality and marginalization within the college football hierarchy. Teams outside the power conferences found themselves at a distinct disadvantage, facing insurmountable odds and a glaring lack of opportunities to compete for the national title. The limited access and narrow pathway to the championship stage not only undermined the ethos of inclusivity and fair play but also stifled the growth and recognition of emerging programs striving to make their mark on the national stage.

The BCS's complex bowl game selection process frequently resulted in controversial and mismatched bowl matchups, diluting the excitement and competitive fervor associated with postseason play. The emphasis on preserving traditional bowl affiliations and contractual obligations often superseded the need for compelling, evenly matched games, leaving fans disillusioned and disengaged with the spectacle of college football's postseason. As lopsided matchups proliferated and the allure of the bowl season waned, the BCS system inadvertently perpetuated a culture of predictability and disenchantment, robbing college football of the spectacle and drama that define its essence.

The culmination of mounting pressure and a resolute commitment to revitalizing college football's championship selection process catalyzed the transition from the BCS to the College Football Playoff (CFP) in 2014. The CFP's inception marked a watershed moment in the sport's history, signaling a departure from the BCS's convoluted and contentious legacy and heralding a new era of transparency, objectivity, and heightened competitive fervor. By embracing a more inclusive and structured playoff format, the CFP sought to address the BCS era's inherent flaws and restore the faith and enthusiasm of the college football community, paving the way for a more vibrant and equitable future for the sport.

Among the primary driving forces behind the inception of the playoff system was the persistent demand for equitability and an objective means of determining the best team in the nation. Advocates of the playoff system contended that it would promote fair competition, offering every qualified team an opportunity to vie for the prestigious national title on the field, rather than through subjective assessments.

Moreover, the financial implications of a playoff system also loomed large. With television networks and sponsors seeking more engaging and revenue-generating matchups, the introduction of a playoff system promised heightened viewership, advertising revenue, and enhanced marketability for the sport. This confluence of sporting integrity and economic viability fueled the push for a comprehensive restructuring of the championship selection process.

The evolution of public opinion played a pivotal role in propelling the college football playoff system to the forefront of discussions within the sports community. As the digital age ushered in an era of instant communication and widespread access to information, fans, players, and pundits alike found a platform to voice their grievances and rally for change. Social media, online forums, and sports-centric websites became breeding grounds for impassioned debates, highlighting the pressing need for a more inclusive and transparent playoff structure.

Simultaneously, the rise of college football as a cultural phenomenon intensified the scrutiny on the existing system's shortcomings. Viewership records shattered, stadium attendance soared, and the fervor surrounding college football reached unprecedented heights, amplifying the significance of addressing the long-standing concerns with the championship selection process.

The CFP introduced a structured, four-team playoff format, wherein the top four teams in the country would compete in semifinal matchups, with the winners progressing to the championship game. This format not only allayed concerns regarding fairness and objectivity but also infused a newfound excitement and anticipation into the culmination of each college football season. The inclusion of a selection committee, comprising esteemed individuals from the world of college football, further enhanced the credibility and transparency of the CFP, garnering widespread approval and acclaim from fans and experts alike.

As the college football playoff system firmly entrenched itself in the fabric of the sport, its impact reverberated far beyond the confines of the playing field. The legacy of the playoff system transcended mere championship determinations, embodying the resilience and adaptability of college football in the face of evolving challenges and aspirations. Its implementation sparked a resurgence of enthusiasm, intensified rivalries, and elevated the quality of gameplay, ushering in a new era of competitiveness and spectacle within the sport.

College Football will continue to grow and evolve. Efforts to mitigate injuries, particularly traumatic head and brain injuries, along with desires to grow the game will undoubtedly bring new and innovative ideas for the century that comes.

There was no way of knowing where the game would be a century and a half later for the initial players, coaches, managers and fans of the 1870s. The next century and a half will feature its own Pop Warners, Jim Thorpes and Walter Camps. There is one thing that seems certain for College Football- it is not going anywhere anytime soon.

RESOURCES

1. Watterson, John Sayle. College Football: History, Spectacle, Controversy. JHU Press, 2001.
2. Bowlby, Alexander. The College Football Championship: Controversy, Tragedy, and a Playoff System. McFarland, 2018.
3. Davis, Parke H. Football, the Ivy League, and the American University: A Study in Institutional Change. University of Michigan Press, 2019.
4. Mandel, Stewart. The Thinking Fan's Guide to College Football. Simon & Schuster, 2014.
5. Blevins, Dave. College Football Traditions and Rivalries: Chants, Pranks, and Pageantry. Globe Pequot, 2012.
6. Galbraith, John S. The Origins of American Football: College, Professionals, and the First Contest. University of Illinois Press, 2019.
7. Rader, Benjamin G. American Sports: From the Age of Folk Games to the Age of Televised Sports. Prentice Hall, 2012.
8. Thamel, Pete. The Rise of the College Football Playoff. Ballantine Books, 2020.
9. Roberts, Randy. A Place on the Team: The Triumph and Tragedy of Title IX. Houghton Mifflin, 2005.
10. Official NCAA Website. "History of College Football." www.ncaa.com.

ABOUT THE AUTHOR

Tim Cooper lives with his family in Central Kentucky. He is the author of GameDay: The Untold Story of College Football (Willard & Arthur Books 2023), Awestruck (Wipf & Stock 2011) and Miles Past Normal (Wipf & Stock 2010). He is the Host of Small Towns Big Ideas Podcast from Cooper Media Group. To get in touch with Tim visit his website: coopermedia.group

Made in United States
Orlando, FL
28 November 2023